P9-DBL-293

FabJob Guide to
Become a
Motivational
Speaker

TAG GOULET

FABJOB GUIDE TO BECOME A MOTIVATIONAL SPEAKER
by Tag Goulet

ISBN 978-1-894638-46-3

Copyright Notice: This edition copyright © 2008 by FabJob Inc. All rights reserved. No part of this work may be reproduced or distributed in any form or by any means (including photocopying, recording, online or email) without the written permission of the publisher. (First edition copyright © 2000 by FabJob Inc.)

Library and Archives Canada Cataloguing in Publication

Goulet, Therese, 1959-
FabJob Guide to become a motivational speaker / Tag Goulet.

Accompanied by CD-ROM.
Includes bibliographical references.
ISBN 1-894638-46-8

1. Public speaking—Vocational guidance. 2. Motivation (Psychology)
I. Title. II. Title: Become a motivational speaker.
PN4129.15.G69 2005   808.5′1′023   C2005-903603-6

Important Disclaimer: Although every effort has been made to ensure this guide is free from errors, this publication is sold with the understanding that the authors, editors, and publisher are not responsible for the results of any action taken on the basis of information in this work, nor for any errors or omissions. The publishers, and the authors and editors, expressly disclaim all and any liability to any person, whether a purchaser of this publication or not, in respect of anything and of the consequences of anything done or omitted to be done by any such person in reliance, whether whole or partial, upon the whole or any part of the contents of this publication. If expert advice is required, services of a competent professional person should be sought.

About the Websites Mentioned in this Guide: Although we aim to provide the information you need within the guide, we have also included a number of websites because readers have told us they appreciate knowing about sources of additional information. (**TIP:** Don't include a period at the end of a web address when you type it into your browser.) Due to the constant development of the Internet, websites can change. Any websites mentioned in this guide are included for the convenience of readers only. We are not responsible for the content of any sites except FabJob.com.

FabJob Inc.
19 Horizon View Court
Calgary, Alberta, Canada T3Z 3M5

FabJob Inc.
4616 25th Avenue NE, #224
Seattle, Washington, USA 98105

To order books in bulk phone 403-949-2039
To arrange a media interview phone 403-949-4980

www.FabJob.com

Contents

About the Author

Tag Goulet has helped thousands of individuals to launch and grow their careers as speakers, seminar presenters and adult educators. As owner of a national seminar company for five years, Tag hired many speakers and taught the popular program "Build Your Career in Speaking and Seminars." For over 10 years she has been teaching public speaking as a part-time university instructor.

Tag herself has spoken before hundreds of thousands of people in dozens of cities over the past 15 years. She has:

- presented business seminars through three seminar companies including American Management Association International
- been hired to speak at a variety of conferences
- facilitated personal growth seminars
- taught continuing education classes
- presented training programs for corporations

Tag has appeared on hundreds of television and radio programs throughout North America and been interviewed for many newspaper and magazine stories. She is the author of *Recipe for Success*, a motivational CD-ROM on goal-achieving distributed in 65 countries, and is a contributor to more than a dozen books including *USA Today* and Amazon bestsellers.

Tag is currently co-CEO of FabJob Inc., an award-winning publishing company named "the #1 place to get published online" by *Writer's Digest*. As a leading career expert, she has written career articles which have been published at top sites including AOL, CNN, and Microsoft's MSN.com. Her career advice has also been featured in media from ABC to Oprah.com and stories at the *Wall Street Journal* and *Entrepreneur Magazine* sites.

Acknowledgements

The book you are reading is the result of knowledge, advice, and feedback shared by a group of talented people.

In this book you will learn from the experiences of numerous professional speakers. While a few stories are told anonymously, a number of successful speakers have kindly shared step-by-step advice to help you achieve your own success in this career. Their names and websites appear elsewhere in this guide.

Throughout the book you will read advice from **Clayton Warholm**, who was my partner in owning a seminar company for five years and has been my husband and partner in life for over 15 years. He is a former regional director of the Canadian Management Centre and American Management Association International, and has hired many speakers. An award-winning speaker, he is a university guest lecturer on public speaking.

Excellent advice also comes from **Dave Brandt**, who wrote the information in this book on how to write a speech. Dave's contributions also appear in a number of other parts of the book.

FabJob Managing Editor **Jennifer James** helped develop this book and organized it so the information would be most useful for the reader. FabJob Editor **Brenna Pearce** provided updated material for the 2008 edition.

FabJob editorial assistants and interns who provided helpful assistance with this book include **Christine Compo-Martin, Jessica Gassmann, Erica Halstead** and **Nadine-Rae Leavell**.

1. Introduction

As the voice comes over the loudspeaker, the room falls silent. Some heads are bowed. Others are tilted upwards. The only sound is the static of the loudspeaker and the powerful voice booming over it. I feel goose-bumps rise on my arms as Dr. Martin Luther King Jr.'s famous "I have a dream" speech begins. When the recording ends, it is clear that no one in the room has been unaffected, although it has been more than 40 years since Dr. King delivered his famous speech.

Throughout history, great speakers have literally changed the world. Dr. King did it. So did Jesus Christ, Nelson Mandela and Mahatma Gandhi. Elizabeth Cady Stanton's reading of the Woman's Bill of Rights began the movement that eventually gave women the right to vote. President John F. Kennedy's speech that one day man would stand on the moon made people believe what had once been impossible. Business leaders such as

Anita Roddick, founder of The Body Shop, are known almost as much for their powerful speeches as they are for their management skills.

It is no wonder that some of the brightest and most talented people in the world dream of becoming speakers. As the preceding examples show, many people famous for their speech-making have been leaders in fields such as politics, business, or religion. However, people from a variety of backgrounds have been able to make an impact as professional speakers.

Some successful professional speakers are former Olympic athletes or Fortune 500 CEOs, but many others come from more humble backgrounds. Before becoming speakers, they may have been stay-at-home moms, small business owners, or even students who dared to dream of having a fabulous, rewarding career as a professional speaker. Information about many successful speakers and some of the techniques they have used to achieve their success is included throughout this guide.

No matter what your background, this guide will give you the information you need to become a speaker who makes a difference.

1.1   What Is a Motivational Speaker?

Just as the job title suggests, a *speaker* is anyone who is paid to speak in front of an audience. A *motivational speaker* aims to motivate audience members to overcome challenges, achieve their dreams, and improve their life.

Even if you are a beginner, you may already have some speaking experience under your belt. For example, have you ever:

- Made a class presentation?
- Given a toast at a wedding reception?
- Trained a group of new staff members?
- Done a reading at your church or house of worship?
- Spoken at a meeting of a club or association?

If you have experience with these or any other types of public speaking, you have already taken the first step towards a career in this field. This guide will help you get paid for what you have been doing for free.

Speakers are hired by companies, conference organizers, associations, and other groups to speak at conventions, seminars, meetings, dinners, and other events. In chapter 7 of this guide you will find details about the various organizations that hire speakers, including contact information for potential employers.

Usually, a speaker is hired by an organization to do a single presentation, which may range in length from 20 minutes to one or more days. (Excellent speakers may be invited back for future presentations.) For those who prefer the security of a regular paycheck, there is the opportunity to earn a steady part-time or full-time income as a "trainer" for a seminar company. Details about what a speaker does, rates of pay, and potential employers are included throughout the guide.

1.2   Benefits of a Speaking Career

There are many reasons why speaking is a popular career choice. The benefits of a speaking career include:

No Experience Is Necessary

The speaking business is one that almost anyone can enter. No special education, experience, or connections are needed to get started and succeed. (In this guide we will show you how to get experience, and explain how to make those important career connections.)

Low Cost to Get Started

Unlike other occupations that can cost thousands of dollars to enter, you can become a speaker no matter what your current financial situation.

High Income Potential

Successful established speakers earn up to $10,000 or more for a single keynote (20-60 minute) speech. A talented beginner can earn as much as $1,000 per speech.

Booming Industry

The speaking business is a multi-billion dollar a year industry. Although speaking jobs are rarely advertised, there are plenty of opportunities for newcomers. (In this guide we will show you how to find out about those unadvertised jobs.)

Opportunity to Make a Difference

Speakers can inspire, motivate, and uplift. They can help businesses and individuals to achieve greater success.

Excitement

Many people consider speaking to be a glamorous career (although, like all "glamorous" careers, it can involve hard work). As a speaker you are the center of attention during your presentation, and you may receive gifts and invitations as "part of the job."

Opportunity to Meet People

People are attracted to speakers who make an impression on them. As a speaker, you may meet interesting people you would not otherwise meet.

Opportunity to Travel

While some speakers prefer to remain in their home community, others have the opportunity to travel around the country or around the world.

Freedom

As a speaker, you are no longer part of the nine-to-five grind. Even if you have steady work through a seminar company, you can usually take time off when you want to.

If you become a self-employed speaker working for a variety of organizations, you can speak on the topics that interest you, and turn down work you don't want. You can even work from home when you are not speaking.

If any of these benefits interest you, read on to find out how this guide can help you succeed as a motivational speaker.

1.3 Inside This Guide

A student who wanted to know the secret to achieving success went to a wise woman who had studied the lives of successful people from all walks of life, including business leaders, explorers, inventors and, of course, motivational speakers.

"Oh, wise woman, what is the secret of success?" asked the student.

"Good judgment," she answered without hesitation.

"How do I get good judgment?" asked the student.

"Experience," said the wise woman.

"But how do I get experience?" asked the student.

"Bad judgment," she replied.

This story is based on a quote attributed to many wise people (including Rita Mae Brown, Will Rogers, and Anthony Robbins) that says the good judgment that comes from experience is often the result of learning from our mistakes. In this guide my goal is to help you avoid common mistakes so you can achieve the success you want more quickly.

If you are experienced as a paid speaker, this guide will help you achieve greater success. If you are a beginner, this guide will give you what you need to get started. Even if you have never spoken in public before, this guide will show you many opportunities to gain experience and break into this industry.

Following a brief introduction, chapter 2 covers some important preliminary steps to prepare you for becoming a motivational speaker. The remaining chapters of the *FabJob Guide to Become a Motivational Speaker* also cover:

Speechwriting

You will get tips for writing your speeches and discover how to get speeches written for you if you don't want to write them yourself. A complete sample motivational speech is included on the CD-ROM that accompanies this guide.

Speaking Skills

This chapter describes the traits of a successful professional speaker and gives suggestions to help you improve your own speaking skills.

Rates of Pay

You will discover how to set your fees, and learn ways to increase your income.

Getting Hired

These information-packed chapters are the heart of the guide. They share industry secrets with advice on:

- Who is hiring (including opportunities speaking for seminar companies, corporations, continuing education departments, conventions, cruise ships, colleges, schools, and more)

- What each type of employer wants

- The best ways to approach potential employers

- How to get potential employers to approach you

- The easiest ways for beginners to break in

- How to improve your odds of getting hired

- How to get paid by organizations with "no money"

Speakers Bureaus

In this chapter you will learn about people who can find work for you.

Setting Up a Speaking Business

This chapter includes information on where to get free advice and assistance.

Being Successful on the Job

In the final chapter of this guide you will discover a number of ways to increase your business including advice about how to put on successful public seminars.

And more!

This book includes many ideas to help you achieve even greater success in this exciting career.

If you are a beginner and want to get the most from this guide, we suggest you read through it all.

If you are an experienced speaker, you may want to skim certain sections. However, we think you will find some valuable information even where you don't expect it. For example, even if you know what topics you want to speak on, the ideas in the section on how to come up with topics could substantially increase your income.

So let's get started...

2. Getting Ready

This chapter includes the following "preliminaries" to becoming a successful motivational speaker:

- Come up with speaking topics
- Develop your areas of expertise
- Create speech titles
- Check out your competition
- Identify your benefits
- Know your audiences

TIP: You can skip this chapter if you plan to work for a company that hires people to present programs the company has already developed. However, if you want to increase your earnings through freelance speaking engagements, you will need to take care of the following preliminaries.

2.1 Come Up with Speaking Topics

Even if you already know exactly what you want to speak about, it is recommended you read the following information about how to develop speaking topics, and refer to this section from time to time in the future.

There are three reasons you may still find this information valuable if you already have decided on your topics:

It May Increase Your Income

Reading this section may help spark some additional ideas. You may discover sources of potential speaking income that you had not previously considered.

You May Need to Change Topics in Future

Even if the topics you would like to speak about now turn out to be wildly popular, at some point in the future you may need to come up with new ones. Why? Because audiences' wants and needs change. Ask any speaker who made a healthy income in 1999 by speaking about Y2K (computer challenges dealing with the start of the year 2000). By January 1, 2000, Y2K was no longer a hot topic simply because most people no longer felt they needed information about it.

Being prepared to shift gears and speak on a new topic will help you stay profitably employed as a speaker. Even the most famous speakers and authors change direction. For example, Barbara De Angelis, speaker and author of numerous relationship books, now focuses on the topic of spirituality.

Your Chosen Topics May Not Sell Well

The third and final reason for knowing how to develop new speaking topics is because the topic you have chosen simply may not sell. You may love it. Your friends may love it. Everyone you have tested the idea on may love it. But when you try to sell it, the people who make the decision about whether to hire you may not love it. If your Plan A topic doesn't sell, be prepared to do something else. Have a Plan B, Plan C, or Plan D waiting in the wings.

2.1.1   What Types of Topics Are Motivational?

Motivational speakers talk on a wide variety of topics to a wide variety of audiences. You could talk to an audience of young people about:

- Staying in school

- Setting goals

- Doing well in school

- Preparing for a career after graduation

- Developing leadership skills

Or you could speak about making positive choices to help them say no to drugs, stay out of gangs, avoid teenage pregnancy, or any number of other things.

Your speeches might help motivate adult audience members to:

- Follow their dreams

- Achieve their goals

- Sell more products

- Improve their relationships

- Develop a positive attitude

- Deal effectively with change

- Work well as part of a team

- Have more fun in life

- Provide excellent customer service

- Improve their health

- Reduce stress

- Achieve financial freedom

- Or anything else that can improve their lives

This is only a small sampling of what you could talk about. In fact, there are hundreds of possible topics you could speak on. The information that follows will help you quickly come up with some specific ideas of your skills, interests, and experiences. Then, the section that comes after will help you focus your lists into topics that are ideal for you.

2.1.2   Do a Skills Inventory

To do a skills inventory, you simply make a list of the things you know how to do. These are your "skills."

If you are like most humans, you know how to do thousands of things. Obviously, you would not try to list all of them.

Instead, what you will list are skills you have that many other people do not have. These skills, which might also be called your "talents" or "unique abilities," are the things you know how to do that other people would like to learn. Virtually all of us have unique abilities. The key is to discover which of your abilities are sufficiently in demand to be turned into speaking topics.

> TIP: The way to discover which skills you have that others want for themselves is to pay attention to the feedback you receive from the world around you.

What Do You Receive Compliments About?

Perhaps friends tell you they admire your ability to tell a great joke or to talk your way out of a traffic ticket. Maybe co-workers have commented on your organizational or leadership skills.

What Do People Ask You to Do?

Are you frequently "nominated" for particular roles in your workplace or among family or friends? Even if you do not see yourself as especially talented, the people in your life are constantly showing you the gifts they see in you.

What Do People Seek Your Advice About?

An excellent way to discover which of your skills are most marketable from a speaking point of view is to examine which ones people seek your guidance about. If people frequently ask to "pick your brain" about something, chances are you have knowledge that others are eager to acquire.

In addition to the skills others see in you, you may have skills others are not aware of simply because you have not used them in a while. There may be a number of talents you picked up through school, volunteer work, hobbies, or past social activities.

For example, you might be good with children or pets; have a flair for writing; know how to talk people into donating to a good cause; have a green thumb; or have an ability to decorate.

Spend some time now making a list of all your skills that come to mind. Do not censor your list as you write it. You can narrow the list down later. For now, include all the talents you can think of.

2.1.3   Do a Life Experience Inventory

The next step in coming up with topics is to make a list of your significant life experiences. This list will help you come up with topics and help you remember some stories you can include in your speeches.

Significant life experiences go deeper than your skills. A *life experience* is any important goal you have achieved or obstacle you have overcome. Your life experiences can be a source of inspiration to others. It is particularly important for motivational speakers to have a wealth of personal experiences they can speak about.

List Goals You Have Achieved

A good place to start when making a list of your life experiences is with goals you have achieved. Have you ever:

- Applied and been hired for a job you really wanted?

- Found someone to love?

- Graduated from high school or college?

- Overcome a bad habit or addiction?

- Successfully started a business?

- Saved enough money to buy something you really wanted (like a home)?

- Received an important promotion?

- Successfully raised children?

You can probably think of many other things you have achieved. Of course, it's even better if you have achieved something extraordinary, such as winning an Olympic medal, publishing a bestselling book, or giving birth to septuplets! But even accomplishments that may seem "ordinary" can provide material for speeches.

What Makes an Experience Powerful

What makes "ordinary" life experiences come alive in a speech is hearing how someone overcame adversity to achieve their dreams.

Graduating from college is something that thousands of people do every year. However, if you single-handedly raised a young family while putting yourself through school, your story can demonstrate a triumph of the human spirit in the face of hardship.

W Mitchell is a successful motivational speaker who has achieved tremendous success despite being badly burned in a motorcycle accident and then paralyzed in a plane crash. You can read more about him at **www.wmitchell.com**.

Chances are you have not had to face the kind of challenges that W Mitchell has experienced in his life. Nevertheless, what you have achieved in spite of the obstacles we all face as humans could be a source of inspiration to others.

Some of the obstacles many people have faced in their lives are:

- Loneliness

- Financial hardship

- Rejection

- Conflict

- Fear

- Loss of employment

- Depression

- Missed opportunities

- Loss of a loved one

Sharing our stories helps us to see that we are not alone, and that it is possible to grow from adversity. For example, millions of people have overcome fear and rejection to find a mate. This is an "ordinary" life experience. Nevertheless, with my partner and husband Clayton Warholm, I was able to take my experiences in this area and turn them into a program for singles seeking a partner. Over a five-year period we spoke at conferences and presented singles workshops more than 200 times in 19 cities. At the heart of my presentations was my own story:

> Only two weeks after my first marriage ended, it was widely reported in the news media that a research study had discovered a drastic shortage of single men in North America. This study was reported on the cover of *Newsweek* magazine, on the front page of the *New York Times*, and in almost every women's magazine. It was even discussed in the movie *Sleepless in Seattle*.

> It was reported that the man shortage was so great that a never-married 40-year-old woman had a greater chance of being in a terrorist attack than she did of getting married! (In case you're wondering, it later turned out the study was based on faulty data.)

> As a newly single woman, this caused me a great deal of fear. I wanted to remarry, but fear made me desperate. During my first year of being single again, I managed to go on three dates, and at the end of each date I heard those three unforgettable words:

"I'll call you."

Audiences would sympathize as they recognized some of their own challenges in our stories. However, we didn't leave it at that.

> **TIP:** Audiences don't want to pay just to hear about your troubles. (Many people are happy to share their troubles for free!) Audiences want to hear how you overcame your obstacles so they can take away some lessons for their own lives.

After describing the challenges we faced, Clayton and I would talk about how we met and married, and give the audience practical advice on how to create their own loving relationships. We took a common life experience and turned it into a popular speaking program. Chances are you have many life experiences you could do the same with.

Even if you don't end up sharing particular personal stories with an audience, making a list of your life experiences can help remind you of how far you have already come in your life and that you can achieve your dreams – like becoming a motivational speaker – when you put your mind to it.

2.1.4   Do an Interests Inventory

Wouldn't you love to speak on a topic you are passionate about? Well, you can – even if it's something you don't have any personal experience with yet. The fact that you are interested in a topic probably means there are others who are also interested and would like to learn more about it.

Depending on your topic, you may be able to learn enough to become an "almost instant" expert. Some speakers have found that investing two solid weeks of research can teach them enough about a topic to be able to present it to an audience with confidence and answer questions intelligently.

Of course, it depends on what your topic is. Two weeks of research won't give you enough information to teach brain surgery to medical students or explain to a group of NASA scientists how to build a space shuttle. However, with two weeks of research you could capably speak on challenges in health care or developments in the space program to a lay (i.e. non-expert) audience.

So make a list of your interests, whether they include animal rights, arbitration, or ancient civilizations. Some of them may end up being suitable for your speeches.

2.1.5   Find Out What's Hot

If you can identify hot topics before your competitors do, you will have a distinct advantage in marketing yourself as a speaker.

A way to spot trends is through the mass media. For example, you could read or skim a newspaper every day (*USA Today* is great), check out the topics of TV talk shows and newsmagazines, and notice which magazines are selling at your local newsstand.

While you're at the newsstand, pick up a copy of *Entertainment Weekly* magazine. *EW* publishes news about entertainment trends and has "top ten" lists of the most popular books, movies, television shows, DVDs, CDs, and Internet sites. The magazine can help you spot emerging trends. For example, a few years ago *EW* published a story about the many books focusing on spirituality. A savvy speaker would have identified this as a hot topic for workshops and seminars.

There are many other magazines (such as *Fast Company*) that describe what's hot. Pick up a few magazines at your newsstand and skim them to see if you can spot trends that would make good speech topics.

2.1.6   Brainstorm for Ideas

If you have ever done a brainstorming session with a group of people, you probably know that it can be an effective way to come up with some wildly creative ideas. Ninety-eight percent of the ideas may not amount to much, but the other two percent of them can be amazing.

Brainstorming usually involves sitting down with a group (perhaps your friends and family members who support you in becoming a speaker) and a challenge (like "come up with speaking topics"), and having everyone toss out ideas while one person writes them down.

For best results, a brainstorming session should start with about 15-20 minutes of idea generation. During this time, group members should be encouraged to share every idea that pops into their head, even if they think it's ridiculous. On reflection, you might discover that an idea that initially sounded ridiculous is actually a good one. Or it just might spark a great idea from someone else in the group.

Explain that no idea is to be evaluated until the end of the idea-generating stage. After all, how many people will be willing to share an outrageously creative idea if they might hear "That's ridiculous!" or see people rolling their eyes in response. Remember: the more outrageous people can be, the more likely you are to come up with some wonderful ideas.

2.2 Develop Your Areas of Expertise

After doing some of the exercises to come up with speaking topics, you may find yourself with a list of 100 or more topics you could speak on. Now it's time to narrow your list down to one or a few areas of expertise. (A single area of expertise is also called a "niche.")

You may question why you need to narrow your list down. After all, you may be wondering, won't you get more work if you can speak on more topics? In fact, exactly the opposite may happen. To see why, put yourself in the shoes of the person who can hire you.

Imagine you are a member of an organization's Executive Committee who has the task of hiring a speaker to give the talk at your annual meeting. The event is less than a month away, but you've been busy so you haven't had time to find a speaker. You have just about given up and asked someone else on the Executive Committee to find the speaker, when you meet Pat Talker at a party:

YOU: So what do you do, Pat?

PAT: I'm a speaker.

YOU: Really??? *(You are instantly interested. This could be the answer to your prayers.)* What kind of speaking do you do?

PAT: Oh, I'll do any kind of speaking.

YOU: I mean, what topics do you speak on?

PAT: I can speak about anything. You tell me what the topic is and I'll speak on it.

YOU: Uh, okay. Well what kind of speeches have you given in the past?

PAT: I haven't done a lot of speaking, but I'm sure I could speak on anything.

Pat may be sure – but would you be? If you are like most people, you would probably doubt that Pat could really deliver. Most of us don't want to hire someone who says they can do "anything." We want to hire experts – people who specialize in delivering what we need.

To see the truth in this, imagine you need to hire a brain surgeon. Would you prefer the doctor who specializes in brain surgery, or the one who says they can do anything ("Just tell me what you need surgery on – which body part did you say that was? – and I'll take care of it")? Wouldn't you run from a doctor who said something like that?

The same principle applies to hiring a speaker. No one wants to hire someone who sounds like an amateur. And that's what Pat sounded like by volunteering the fact that he hadn't spoken a lot but felt he could speak on anything.

Later in this guide, you will read step-by-step information that will help you avoid the "amateur" label. This guide will tell you some simple and creative ways to quickly establish yourself as an expert. Even more importantly, it will tell you what to say when you talk to a potential employer so you sound like the expert they want to hire. For now, start by deciding what you want to be an expert in.

TIP: When choosing your areas of expertise it is important to choose something that people and organizations will pay to hear about.

This may sound obvious, but some speakers develop niches that are simply not saleable. For example, if you speak on "The Biology of African Primates," you are unlikely to find many audiences willing to pay to hear you. You may find audiences, but they will probably expect you to speak for free.

TIP: People are willing to pay for information that will improve their lives. Few people are interested in historical or theoretical information about a subject.

For example, would you have bought this guide if all it contained was a history of public speaking or opinions about who the greatest speakers are? Of course not! You almost certainly bought this guide because of how it will benefit you personally. Most people want information that will improve their lives by:

- Solving their problems

- Helping them achieve their goals

- Entertaining them

- Otherwise contributing to their well-being

So go through your list of topics and look at which ones people would be willing to pay for. Notice if there are certain topic areas that appear repeatedly or that you feel particularly passionate about.

Related topics can be pulled together under the umbrella of a niche, such as "Leadership," "Communications," "Change," or "Personal Development." To see other niches used by successful professional speakers, visit the topics page at **www.speaking.com**. You will notice that many motivational speakers also have other areas of expertise.

2.3   Create Speech Titles

Great speech titles can help you stand out, especially if your niche is crowded with other speakers.

2.3.1   Using More Than One Title Per Speech

There is a story of a man who became a successful speaker by marketing the same speech under 50 different titles. The story probably is not true, since he would have been discovered the first time a client invited him back to deliver a new speech. ("We enjoyed your 'Keys to Success' talk so much, could you come back and give us your 'Winners Never Quit' talk?")

Nevertheless, having a variety of titles can help boost your business as a speaker. The reason is because we humans have different tastes. A potential employer may not be interested in Title X, but will decide that Title Y would be just right for their group. A different potential employer may have exactly the opposite reaction.

When I was hiring speakers for an event, I found Bob Stebbins, a sociology professor who speaks on humor. Among the titles of his speeches are "On the Sociology of Humor" and "Give Me Life, Liberty, and the Pursuit of Laughter."

I hired Bob to deliver the second speech on the basis of its title alone. For all I knew, both speeches were exactly the same. I figured that title would sell more tickets to our event, and I was right. We had a fantastic turnout.

2.3.2 Coming Up With Titles

One way to come up with effective titles of your own is to use the brainstorming technique described in section 2.1.6.

When evaluating your titles, look for those that offer strong benefits to potential employers. "How to" titles (those that promise to teach how to do something) can be particularly powerful. For instance, some of the most popular topics offered by Dr. Tony Alessandra, recognized by *Meetings and Conventions Magazine* as "one of America's most electrifying speakers," are "How to Get and Keep Customers for Life" and "How to Gain the Competitive Advantage in Selling."

But before you start contacting potential employers using a title you have come up with, you should first find out whether or not someone else already owns that title. This means you need to...

2.4 Check Out Your Competition

Your competition is any alternative that potential employers will consider when thinking about hiring you. Usually, "the competition" will be other speakers. There are thousands of speaker web sites which can provide you with information about other speakers.

However, the quickest way to access information about the competition is by visiting sites which list hundreds of speakers. Perhaps the most informative site is **speaking.com**, which provides rates, biographical information, and speech titles for speakers who collectively specialize in hundreds of topics.

You can also check out a list of outstanding professional speakers who are members of the National Speakers Association at **www.nsaspeaker. org**. By visiting the "Find a Speaker" section of the NSA's website, you can search for speakers on a variety of topics, including "motivation." Many of the speakers have websites you can visit.

Speaking "Stars"

You shouldn't be too concerned if you discover a number of "star" speakers in your chosen niche. For example, if you have decided to speak on "leadership," it can be intimidating to see that you will be in competition with renowned leadership experts like Dr. Stephen Covey, author of *The 7 Habits of Highly Effective People*.

However, the reality is that you are not going to lose all your potential speaking engagements to Dr. Covey. He could not possibly deliver speeches to all the thousands of organizations that want leadership speakers each year. Plus, most organizations can not afford the "$50,000 and over" fee that Dr. Covey charges. Assuming you are willing to speak for less than $50,000, you will be dealing with an entirely different set of potential employers.

Even if you are not competing directly with the speaking stars, it is useful to see what these speakers do to market themselves. It may give you some good ideas for marketing yourself.

Among the speaking superstars are the following (listed in alphabetical order): Les Brown, Jack Canfield, Mark Victor Hansen, Tom Peters, Jeanne Robertson, Anthony Robbins, Jim Rohn, Brian Tracy, Denis Waitley, and Zig Ziglar. You can find more information about these speakers online by looking up their names in your favorite search engine. (Many speakers use their name as their domain name, e.g. **www.anthony robbins.com** or **www.briantracy.com**.)

Twenty other speaking stars – including Tony Alessandra, Dianna Booher, Jim Cathcart, Patricia Fripp, and Nido Qubein – have formed an association called Speakers Roundtable. You can read about them and find links to their websites at **www.speakersroundtable.com/ speakers.html**.

Free Speakers

Another type of competition you should consider is the free speaker. For example, organizations such as Alcoholics Anonymous provide schools with speakers free of charge, so if you want to speak to school children about the dangers of alcohol abuse, you have to offer something special.

No matter who your competition is, what matters to potential employers is how you are different from or better than your competitors. In the case of star speakers, one difference is how much less expensive you are! When it comes to competing with speakers in your league, you can distinguish yourself by showing potential employers all the benefits of hiring you.

2.5 Identify Your Benefits

What convinces people to book speakers is a belief that they will receive value for their money. Your benefits are the value people receive from hearing you speak.

Some speakers make the mistake of confusing the benefits of their presentations with features, such as the content. For example, a speaker might say, "I offer the audience information about interpersonal communication skills." While it is fine to say this, it does not go far enough.

People want to know how they will benefit from hearing the contents. For example, if you state that your audience members will learn how to say "no" so they can avoid burnout, "avoiding burnout" is a benefit of hearing you speak.

The following example can help you remember the difference between benefits and features:

Imagine you are driving down the highway one evening. It is getting late so you are starting to think about finding a hotel for the night. As you drive, you see a billboard for a hotel with "22 rooms" written in large letters. Aside from the hotel name and address, there is no other information on the sign. How interested would you be in that hotel?

Now imagine as you continue driving you see a billboard for a different hotel, which says "Our quiet rooms and comfortable beds ensure you will get a restful night's sleep." Wouldn't you be more interested in the hotel advertised on the second billboard? Of course you would!

This illustrates the difference between features (such as "22 rooms") and benefits (such as "a restful night's sleep"). Benefits sell.

As Anthony Robbins says, people typically take action either to avoid pain or to gain pleasure. Your speeches should therefore offer individuals and organizations ways to gain pleasure (the first three examples below) or avoid pain (the last three examples):

- How to increase your profits

- How to find the love of your life

- How to achieve peace of mind

- How to keep your customers

- How to resolve conflicts with your teenagers

- How to keep your best employees

All of the above are examples of information that will improve people's lives. Make sure that your own benefits offer the same. To illustrate this point, which of the following speeches do you think is most marketable, "The History of Public Relations" or "How to Get Free Publicity"?

The answer, of course, is "How to Get Free Publicity," which offers a benefit (getting free publicity). However, the title alone may not be enough to convince someone to hire you.

2.5.1 Answer the "So What?" Question

A potential employer who doesn't have experience with publicity could look at the title and say "So what? Why would the people attending my conference care whether or not they get free publicity?"

You can answer the "so what?" question with a list of additional benefits that the people hearing you will receive. To illustrate with the above example, here is how you might explain some benefits of getting free publicity to potential employers.

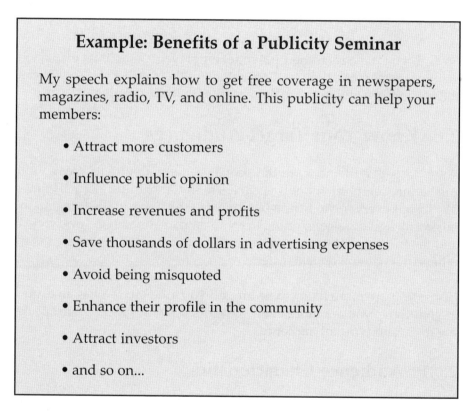

Example: Benefits of a Publicity Seminar

My speech explains how to get free coverage in newspapers, magazines, radio, TV, and online. This publicity can help your members:

- Attract more customers

- Influence public opinion

- Increase revenues and profits

- Save thousands of dollars in advertising expenses

- Avoid being misquoted

- Enhance their profile in the community

- Attract investors

- and so on...

The point is to include all the benefits you believe will be of value to the audience that would hear you speak.

As you go through the exercise of identifying your benefits, keep asking yourself, "So what?" Remember that a benefit that is obvious to you (such as "get free publicity") may not be obvious to the person thinking of hiring you.

2.5.2   Give People What They Want

Even more important than clearly communicating your benefits is ensuring that your benefits are what the audience actually wants and needs.

Let's say, for example, that your niche is customer service, and you want to offer a speech on how to attract more customers. If you approach an organization of business owners who already have more customers than they can handle, your speech will almost certainly be of no interest to them. However, they would probably be interested in a speech on how to keep customers happy during a time of rapid business growth.

So once you have identified potential employers (as will be explained below), spend some time finding out about their problems, so you can offer them the solutions (i.e. the benefits) that they want and need.

2.6   Know Your Target Audiences

Your "target" audiences are the people you are aiming to speak to. It can be very tempting for new speakers to say something along the lines of: "I want everyone to hear what I have to say!" Avoid the temptation. It is costly and time-consuming to try to market yourself to "everyone," and the truth is that some people are bound to be more interested than others in what you have to offer.

Just as you are more likely to be hired if you are perceived as an expert in your topic, you are more likely to be hired if you specialize in speaking to certain types of audiences.

2.6.1   Audience Characteristics

Instead of aiming at everyone, or "the general public," narrow your audience down to distinct groups. Depending on your niche and topics, you may define your primary audience (the people who will actually hear you speak) by characteristics such as:

- Age

- Gender

- Geographic location

- Skill level (e.g. beginners or professionals)

- Occupation

- Industry

- Hobbies or interests

There are a variety of other characteristics that distinguish one group of people from another, and may be important in identifying your audience. For example, if you offer programs for singles, you would obviously include "single marital status" as one of the characteristics of your target audience.

2.6.2   Will They Pay Me to Speak?

When deciding who your audience will be, the most important question to ask is: "Would they be willing to invest the time or money to hear me speak?" The answer will be "yes" if you can provide solutions to their problems.

One way to be viewed as an expert by your audience is to specialize in a particular industry. An industry consists of members of any business or occupational group, such as restaurant owners, hair stylists, bankers, or doctors.

I had the pleasure of hearing a presentation by Jack Canfield, co-creator of the *Chicken Soup for the Soul* books, and one of the things I learned from him is that if you specialize in speaking to a particular industry, it may take 10 years before your market is saturated to the point where you would have to move on. He speaks from firsthand experience. Although Jack Canfield is now a renowned authority on self-esteem and peak performance, he used to present speeches to chiropractors on topics such as "How to get one new patient per day."

Whether or not you choose to specialize in a particular industry, it is important to identify your potential audiences so you can market to them most effectively.

It is also important to realize that your audience includes both the people who will attend your speeches *and* the people who will hire you. You need to be able to convince both groups of the value of hearing you speak. Each group will also have different ideas about what constitutes a "benefit." The people who will attend your speeches are most interested in the types of benefits described in section 2.5.

The people who will hire you expect a number of additional benefits. For example, they want:

- A speaker who is easy to work with

- No unexpected expenses

- To look good for having hired you

TIP: A key to getting hired is to emphasize the benefits you offer for the people who can hire you.

3. Speechwriting

For many speakers, writing a speech is more difficult than actually delivering the speech. Fortunately for those who would rather speak than write, you can hire a speechwriter if you would rather not write the speech yourself.

3.1 Hiring a Speechwriter

A number of outstanding speakers do not write their own material. Politicians, company executives, and many other high-profile people routinely have their speeches written by someone else.

In fact, some of the quotes we attribute to famous people were actually penned by speechwriters.

Who wrote it?
"Ask not what your country can do for you –
ask what you can do for your country."

If you answered "President John F. Kennedy," you are correct about who *said* it. But the person who actually wrote it was James C. Humes. Humes, who is now a successful speaker himself, is the author of *Confessions of a White House Ghostwriter*.

3.1.1 Finding Speechwriters

Here are some ways you can find someone to write a speech for you:

Hire a Public Relations Firm

A public relations firm is a company that provides public relations services to clients. Speechwriting is one of the services provided by many PR firms. Although this is an expensive option (see "Speechwriting costs" on the next page), a public relations firm can work with you to craft a speech that delivers a powerful message.

Because most public relations firms specialize in writing speeches for businesspeople rather than motivational speakers, you may need to shop around to find one that can deliver the type of speech you need. You can find public relations firms in your local Yellow Pages, or do a search for "public relations firm" online.

Hire a Speechwriter

Most public relations firms offer speechwriting as only one of many services. Speechwriters, on the other hand, specialize in writing speeches so they may have more directly related experience.

You can find a number of speechwriters on the Internet by searching for "speechwriting service" at any search engine. Another way to find a good speechwriter is through word of mouth. You may get some recommendations by networking with other speakers through organizations such as the National Speakers Association. Or you may even find another speaker who also provides speechwriting services. Speakers organizations are listed in section 9.3.2 of this book.

Hire a Freelance Writer

A freelance writer with speechwriting experience may be able to provide you with a good speech relatively quickly and inexpensively. You can find freelance writers by placing a classified ad in the help wanted section of your local newspaper. However, you may find many applicants will be inexperienced in actual speechwriting.

Another alternative is to place an ad in a newsletter or online "job bank" through your local chapter of a professional association such as the Public Relations Society of America at **www.prsa.org**, the International Association of Business Communicators at **www.iabc.com** or the Canadian Public Relations Society at **www.cprs.ca**.

When you place a listing with one of these organizations, you will need to specify that the listing is for a part-time contract position.

3.1.2 Speechwriting Costs

There is no "standard" cost to get a speech written. The cost will vary depending on who you hire to write the speech and how much assistance you give them.

For example, if you have already prepared a draft of a 20-minute speech, but you want someone to polish it, a local freelance writer might be able to do that for as little as $100. On the other hand, if you want to hire a large public relations firm to write a 20-minute speech for you from scratch, you might be looking at a bill of $2,000 or more.

Public relations firms and freelance writers typically charge by the hour for their labor. While a freelance writer may charge only $20 per hour, a public relations firm may charge ten times that amount—as much per hour as a good lawyer!

Thus a $2,000 speechwriting fee from a public relations firm might be based on the firm spending 10 hours of time at $200 per hour. However, a speech that might take one firm 10 hours to write might take another firm much longer. One speechwriter says it can take up to 40 hours to prepare a 20-minute presentation, from the initial meeting with the speechwriter to the final draft.

> **TIP:** To avoid a nasty surprise, it's a good idea to negotiate a flat fee rather than an hourly rate. That way, you know the cost will not go over the agreed-upon fee.

Many speechwriters charge by the number of minutes in the speech itself. According to *Writer's Market*, a standard rate for speechwriting is $50-$200 per finished minute, or flat fees ranging from $100 to $3,000 depending on the length and purpose of the speech.

3.1.3   Working With a Speechwriter

Before you hire someone to write a speech for you, it is a good idea to meet with them and ask for references and sample speeches. Many speechwriters will provide an initial consultation free of charge so you can see whether there is a fit between your needs and their services.

During your initial consultation, you should ask the speechwriter plenty of questions. The following are questions you should consider asking.

What Is Your Specialty?

When you contact someone advertising their services as a writer, this is the first question to ask. Some writers specialize in writing articles, news releases, or brochures. You want to find someone who specializes in, or at least has experience with, writing speeches.

How Long Have You Been Writing Speeches?

You don't need someone with 10 years of experience, but they shouldn't be learning how to write speeches by starting with yours.

What Types of Speeches Do You Write?

Most speech writers have plenty of experience writing for corporate CEOs, but may have no experience writing for a professional speaker. If their speeches focus on "thanking everyone for your hard work on our new construction project," they may not know how to write a speech that fires up an audience. Or it could be that their corporate speeches are incredibly inspiring, and they have been itching to write for a motivational speaker.

Do You Have Samples I Can Read?

While the speechwriter may not be able to give you copies of client speeches (which usually belong to the client), they will likely have written some samples for prospective clients.

How Do You Personalize a Speech?

Many of your clients will expect you to personalize your speeches to their particular audience. The speechwriter should know how to make a speech relevant to an audience by including references to people the audience knows and issues they are concerned with. The speechwriter may even give you a list of questions to ask your client.

What Happens If We Decide to Work Together?

This might be a series of questions such as: What do you need from me? How long does it take you to write the speech? How much do you charge? What happens if I think the speech needs changes? (Does it cost extra for revisions?) Will I own the copyright in the speech? (This allows you to use it elsewhere – such as publishing it in a book or on your website – and keeps the speechwriter from recycling it for another speaker.)

Who Can I Call for a Reference?

If possible, see if the speechwriter can refer you to other speakers they have written for. If you know they have written for other speakers, but they don't give them as references, call the speakers anyway to ask their opinion of the speechwriter's services.

As mentioned above, it is also a good idea to ask a speechwriter to quote you a flat fee for writing your speech. This quote should be in writing so there will be no misunderstandings.

Once you start working together, provide your speechwriter with the basic information that you would need if you were preparing your own speech. For example, they will need to know the purpose of the speech, the intended audience, and so on.

3.2 Writing Your Own Speech

If you are going to write your own speeches, you'll want to familiarize yourself with the main parts of the speechwriting process.

- Analyze the audience and the occasion

- Determine the goal of your speech

- Develop a thesis statement

- Find material for your speech

- Organize your material

- Write out your speech

- Add transitions

- Write the introduction and conclusion

- Edit it

In the rest of this chapter you will find some practical tips to help you get started, followed by some resources with further information on speechwriting. The CD-ROM included with this book includes a sample motivational speech.

3.2.1 Before You Begin Writing

There are two very important things you need to think about before you start putting your speech together. These steps will help you determine the overall tone and content of your speech.

Analyze the Audience and the Occasion

Think about the people you will be speaking to, so you can tailor your speech to fit their situation. You wouldn't use a story about Ben Affleck and Jennifer Garner to illustrate a point about relationships if you were speaking to an all-male senior citizen group. However, that example could work well for a mixed audience of singles in their 20s and 30s.

Keep in mind the basic demographics of your audience, such as:

- Age

- Occupation

- Religion

- Ethnic background

- Gender

- Educational background

- Political background

Also consider the external circumstances (time, place, etc.) surrounding your speech. Will you give your speech after a luncheon in July? You may want to include some audience participation or some humor to keep your listeners awake. Are you speaking at a corporate gathering for a department store chain you've shopped at? You can talk about some experiences you've had as one of their customers.

Determine the Goal of Your Speech

The goal of your speech is another factor to consider when thinking about what to say.

Are you mainly trying to entertain your audience? You'll want to include lots of humor and stories, and keep a light tone throughout your speech. Are you trying to inspire your listeners? Give them some profound statements that will make an impression on them. Are you giving an informative speech? Keep your information simple, and use lots of examples and illustrations.

Develop a Thesis Statement

A thesis statement is one sentence that explains exactly what your speech will be about. It will be part of the introduction of your speech, and it sums up the gist of what you're going to say. For instance, a thesis statement might say "I'm going to tell you how improving your people skills will help boost your sales" or "I will show you just how easy it is to start your own business."

All of the information you include in your speech should be related to your thesis statement, so it's a good idea to come up with a thesis before you start gathering material. Sticking to your thesis statement will keep you focused and help you avoid adding irrelevant information.

At this stage, you do not need a perfectly worded thesis statement. If necessary, you can fine-tune it as you do your research, and then rewrite it again when you actually write your introduction.

3.2.2   Find Material for Your Speech

Your Personal Experiences

As a motivational speaker, the first place to look for material is in your own life experiences. This is a key to your credibility as a speaker. People want to hear about how to achieve success or overcome an obstacle from someone who has actually done it – they don't want to hear someone simply discussing how others have done it. I know of one speaker whose personal experiences make up 95 percent of her speeches.

The Importance of Storytelling

A key to using your experiences in a speech effectively is to make a number of them into stories. Audiences are usually not interested in hearing a non-famous person recite a list such as: "I did this, then I did this, then I did this, then this happened, so I did this."

People want drama, they want excitement, they want to be moved and touched. The experiences of your life have all of these elements. The challenge is learning how to communicate in a way that impacts others. If you think about it, you are probably already a storyteller with your friends and family. However, to ensure a story is suitable for an audience that doesn't know and love you, each of the stories in your speech should:

- Be relatively brief (no more than a minute or two)

- Be interesting and "paint a picture" for the audience

- Be something the audience can identify with

- Have a point (the "moral" of the story)

Examples of Stories

A few stories are included in this guide. For example, there is a brief story in section 6.5.2 ("How to Get Employers to Approach You") on the problem of promoting a seminar by distributing flyers door-to-door. In section 6.2 ("A Potential Employer's Greatest Fear") there is a longer story on the hazards of not seeing a speaker before hiring him.

There are many other places you can find examples of stories. Two of the best are *Reader's Digest* magazine (for short stories or anecdotes) and *Chicken Soup for the Soul* books (for longer stories).

Every issue of *Reader's Digest* includes short stories in features such as "Life in These United States" (called "Life's Like That" in Canada) and "All in a Day's Work."

Likewise, reading *Chicken Soup for the Soul* stories can give you a sense of how to write a story that will move an audience. The series was initially created by Jack Canfield and Mark Victor Hansen to share stories they had been giving in their speeches. You can find a few sample stories online at the *Chicken Soup for the Soul* website at **www.chicken soup.com**. While many of the samples at the webpage are too long for a speech, some of them might be adapted, or parts of them adapted, to work well in a speech. Chicken Soup stories are also widely available on the Internet.

Using Other People's Stories in Your Speeches

As you read these stories, or hear others, you may be tempted to use some of them in your speeches. Using a story written by someone else may be fine on occasion, as long as you give credit to the original author. However, the most important stories in your speech should be original.

I remember a new speaker telling me about how she had recently given a speech which concluded with a dramatic story. As she started to tell me the story, I realized it sounded familiar:

An elderly man had given his wife a nightgown which the old woman had never worn. She had been saving it for a special occasion. Now the husband was getting out the nightgown for his beloved wife to wear ... *(dramatic pause)* ... in her coffin.

This story was meant to be extremely moving and teach a moral about not putting things off "for special occasions." However, it didn't have that effect on me because I already knew the ending. Because I had heard it before, only the story was memorable – not the speaker.

Material From Your Client

There are some speakers who deliver the same speech over and over again. For example, Temple University's founder Russell H. Conwell gave his famous "Acres of Diamonds" speech more than 6,000 times.

However, most motivational speakers find that clients expect them to customize their speech. A customized speech has been adapted to the audience and the occasion. It may include references to key people, events, companies, or other details of direct interest to a particular audience. If the speaker delivers the speech again, they would remove those references and include ones of interest to the new audience.

To customize a speech, a speaker needs to obtain information about the occasion and the audience from the person who has hired the speaker. You can find some tips on how to do this later in the guide.

Other Sources of Material

With the growth of the Internet there are now literally millions of potential sources of information. The types of speech material you can use in addition to your own stories includes:

- Factual statements

- Statistics

- Expert opinions

- Quotations

- Humor

- Other people's stories (use sparingly and give credit!)

You can find some of this information through first-hand research; for example, by interviewing experts or conducting surveys. However, most of your material will probably come from secondary sources, such as websites, books, and newspapers.

Online, visit **http://150.208.100.115/uploads/speechweb.htm** for links to historical documents and other references such as *Bartlett's Familiar Quotations*. Other quotation sites, such as **www.quoteland.com** and **www. famous-quotations.com**, contain archives of inspirational quotes on a variety of topics.

When you include this kind of material in your speeches, you will help raise the audience's perception of your credibility. Credibility is an important trait for a speaker to have, and is discussed further in section 4.1.

Cautions About Using Material from Other Sources

Copyright

In many cases you will need permission to use material from another publisher or writer. While it is usually okay to use small portions of someone else's work, you cannot simply use a substantial portion of their material without permission—even if you give them credit.

For example, I remember one speaker telling me that she was planning to write a speech based on a popular book. I cautioned her that doing so could get her into serious legal trouble because it would infringe on the author's copyright. The issue of copyright is explored in more detail in section 3.3.

Accuracy

Another challenge with using material from other sources is that it may be inaccurate. To avoid losing credibility with your audience, make sure any material you use has been verified and is credited to the right source. For example, the following quote is currently circulating on the Internet:

"Our deepest fear is not that we are inadequate. Our deepest fear is that we are powerful beyond measure. It is our light, not our darkness, that most frightens us. We ask ourselves — Who am I to be brilliant, gorgeous, talented, fabulous? Actually, who are you not to be? You are a child of God. Your playing small does not serve the world."

This quote is commonly credited as being an excerpt from Nelson Mandela's inaugural speech. The problem is that Mandela never even said it, let alone wrote it. It actually comes from the book *A Return to Love*, by Marianne Williamson.

Any speaker who mistakenly attributes information risks losing credibility with their audience. Thus, it is a good idea to check a number of sources until you are satisfied that the information is correct.

3.2.3 Organize Your Material

Organizing your material involves putting your points into order. Something that can help you in this task is to use index cards (3" x 5" cards available from any office supplies store). You can write down ideas on the cards, and then rearrange the cards into logical patterns.

A standard speech contains three parts: the introduction, body, and conclusion. The introduction gets the audience's attention and helps you establish a rapport with them. The body consists of the main points or topics you want to cover in your speech. And the conclusion summarizes your main points and leaves the audience with a sense of closure. These parts of a speech will be discussed in more detail in the next section.

You can organize your speech in several ways. The most common patterns are:

- Topical order

- Chronological order

- Spatial order

- Cause and effect

Most speeches are organized in topical order. When you use topical order, you organize your speech according to the main points you want to make. For instance, say you are writing a speech on how to maintain a meaningful relationship. While brainstorming and writing your ideas down on the index cards, you notice that most of your ideas fit into three broader categories (i.e. "Understanding Yourself," "Understanding the Other Person," and "Staying Together"). These three categories would become the three main points of your speech.

You can also organize your speech in chronological order, grouping your main points according to time. For the same speech on relationships, you could talk about a relationship you were in that fell apart ten years ago. Then you could talk about a new relationship that you began five years ago, and discuss what you're doing today to keep this relationship going.

A speech that's organized in spatial order is arranged according to points in space that the audience can visualize. These points can be either literal or figurative. For a literal example, say you've noticed differences in the way that people from Canada, the United States, and England view the dating process. Each country could serve as a main point for your speech. An example of a figurative outline might be to say that relationships fizzle out when both partners are far apart emotionally, while healthy relationships are those where both partners know how to stay close together.

With the cause and effect pattern, you describe something and then talk about what caused it to happen. For instance, you could define what you mean by a meaningful relationship (the effect) and then discuss two or three steps you can take to start a relationship (the causes).

Of course, you aren't limited strictly to these patterns. You can combine any or all of them, or you can organize the speech any way you want to. Just make sure everything you plan to say flows logically from one point to the next. You can see an example in the sample speech included on the CD-ROM with this book.

3.2.4   Write Your Speech

> **NOTE:**   Experienced speakers who are completely familiar with their material can skip this step.

Once you have put the points into a logical order, the next step for many beginning speakers is to write out the complete body of your speech. (The body is everything except the introduction and conclusion, which you will write later.) You will not actually be reading your speech from a written manuscript, but at this stage it can help you ensure that the speech sounds good.

The best way to carry out this step is to write your speech as you speak it. In other words, don't sit down at a computer and silently begin typing. Instead, you should speak aloud – you can even record yourself – and type what you say. The result will be much more natural.

> TIP: People speak at the rate of about 125-150 words per minute, so write the first draft of your speech based on this guideline.

Step #1: Writing the Body

The body is the main part of your speech. It's where you present all the major points that you plan to cover during your speech. Remember, every point you make should relate to your thesis statement. Also remember the organizational pattern that you have chosen and stick to it as you write the body.

Regardless of how talented a speaker you are, your audience isn't likely to remember everything you talk about. They will retain more from your speech if you focus on just a few important themes. A good rule of thumb is to include anywhere from two to five main points.

Use Evidence

As you write, keep a good balance between your own ideas and the material that you're using from other sources. If your entire speech is nothing but quotes from other sources, your audience will be upset because you've said only things they could have looked up themselves.

On the other hand, if your whole speech consists of nothing but your own opinions, your audience won't find you very believable. Don't be afraid to say what you want to say, but make sure you have ample facts, statistics, and stories from other sources to back it up.

Add Transitions

As part of writing the body, you should add some transitions (or "connectives") between each topic. Transitions are comments that let your audience know you are moving on to a new topic. They help your audience "stay with you" and keep them from getting confused, as can happen when a speaker jumps from one topic to another.

A transition can be as simple as saying "Now that we have covered X, let's take a look at Y." However, your speech will be more interesting if you can make one part of your speech seem to flow into another.

Keep it Interesting

Many people get distracted easily. After a few minutes of listening to your speech, some people's minds will begin to wander a little. However, there are things you can do while writing your speech to help prevent this from happening.

Remember, you're writing a speech, not a report. You want your speech to sound friendly and engaging. Write as though you're having a conversation with a friend, not like you're reading from the encyclopedia. Your audience will pay more attention if you talk *to* them, not *at* them.

Humor is another way to keep your audience interested. Audiences respond very favorably to humor, as long as the humor is appropriate and tasteful. Try illustrating your important points with a joke or humorous story.

Of course, a story doesn't always have to be humorous to be interesting. You may have found several non-humorous stories while gathering material for your speech. Consider strategically placing these stories at points in your speech where you want to make sure your audience is paying attention.

Also, work in some visual aids (graphs, props, pictures, etc.) to help your audience see what you're saying. People retain visual images longer than any other kind of stimulus, so using visual aids can help your audience understand and remember what you're saying.

Step #2: Write Your Opening and Closing

After you have written the body of your speech, you can write an opening and closing that will fit with the rest of the speech. (These may also be referred to as the "introduction" and "conclusion.")

Both are critical to the success of your speech. The opening can help to get the audience's attention, establish your credibility, and lead into your talk. The closing can wrap up your speech and leave your audience wanting to hear more from you—something you definitely want as a motivational speaker!

The Introduction

The first 60 seconds of your introduction are the most important 60 seconds of your whole speech. During this short period of time, audience members get their first impression of you and decide whether to listen to you or think about what's for lunch instead. Make these precious seconds count.

Here are some things you can do to get your audience's attention:

- Open with a startling fact or story relating to your topic

- Ask the audience a question (for an added touch, you can have them shout out answers or answer with a show of hands)

- Tell a joke about your topic

- Open with an interesting quote from a well-known expert

- Make reference to the event at which you're speaking

- Anything else you can think of

Once you have your audience's attention, there are three more things you need to do in your introduction. First, you should tell the audience the benefits of listening to you speak (see section 2.5 for a discussion of benefits).

Second, you need to convince the audience that you are qualified to speak on this topic. Doing this can be as simple as mentioning your work history, referring to a personal experience, talking about some research you've done – anything, as long as it illustrates why you're qualified to speak on this particular topic.

And finally, you should include your thesis statement somewhere in your introduction so that your audience knows, in a nutshell, what your speech is going to be about.

The Conclusion

The conclusion is as important as the introduction. Now that your audience has listened to everything you've said, your conclusion should make them feel that it was worth paying attention to you.

An effective conclusion does three things:

• Ties all the elements of your speech together

• Gives the audience a sense of closure

• Leaves the listeners wanting more

In your conclusion, summarize the main points of your speech. You do not need to repeat the points, but make your conclusion restate the main thrust of what you've said.

Also, make sure your conclusion effectively lets the audience know your speech is winding down. Tie up all the loose ends. Your audience will feel confused if you end your speech abruptly.

And finally, your conclusion should leave your audience in an appropriate state of mind for your topic. If you were trying to inspire your audience to boost their sales, your conclusion should leave your audience feeling inspired. If you were trying to show them how to have a meaningful relationship, your conclusion should make them feel like they can start putting your advice into action the minute your speech ends.

If your conclusion pulls together all three of these elements, you're ready for the next step in the speechwriting process.

Step #3: Edit It

Editing can make the difference between an adequate speech and an outstanding one. Once your speech is written, practice delivering it. This will show you whether your speech is the right length, how well it flows, and whether anything sounds awkward. If something doesn't work, then cut it out.

This can be difficult to do. I know from personal experience how hard it is to cut stories you really enjoy out of a speech. However, if they do not directly relate to the speech, or if the speech is too long, you may have to sacrifice some of your material for the good of the speech.

Many of the resources that follow offer some good tips for editing your material. And remember that assistance is available from speechwriters or speaking coaches if you need help editing your material.

3.2.5   Speechwriting Resources

Free Advice

- Patricia Fripp offers some wonderful insights into writing engaging and dynamic speeches. You can find a variety of helpful articles at her website, at **www.fripp.com/articleslist.html**. She also produces a free e-mail newsletter which offers excellent tips.

- Garrett Patterson, a professional speechwriter, offers tips on researching, writing, and performing speeches at **www.nvo.com/speechwriters/tipswritingperformingspeeches/**.

- Good advice is offered by the University of North Carolina's Writing Center at **www.unc.edu/depts/wcweb/handouts/speeches.html**.

- You can also find some excellent advice on a variety of public speaking topics at Allyn and Bacon's Public Speaking Website at **http://wps.ablongman.com/ab_public_speaking_2**.

Sample Speeches

Reading other speeches can help you get a sense of what makes a speech great. You can find some excellent speeches online.

- The History Place has a page which offers a Speech of the Week and a Great Speeches section. You can read the Speech of the Week at **www.historyplace.com/speeches** and the Great Speeches section at **www.historyplace.com/speeches/previous.htm**.

- The Online Speech Bank also has an extensive collection of great speeches, available in both text and audio formats. The site is located at **www.americanrhetoric.com/speechbank.htm**.

If you do not have access to the Internet, visit your local public library to find sample speeches and books on speechwriting. A classic that covers both speechwriting and speaking is Dale Carnegie's *The Quick and Easy Way to Effective Speaking*. Another book you may find helpful is *Writing Great Speeches: Professional Techniques You Can Use*, by Alan M. Perlman.

3.3 Copyright

Copyright legally protects authors of original works – including books, articles, or speeches. Under copyright law, a work cannot be printed or performed without the authorization of the person who wrote it.

As a speaker, copyright is important for two reasons. First, it determines what you can legally use from other sources and, second, it can protect your own speeches from being "stolen" by others.

3.3.1 Copyrighting Your Speeches

When you write a speech, it is protected by copyright law as soon as it is written or recorded. (The law does not protect impromptu speeches for which there is no permanent record.)

You do not have to register your speech to protect it, but registration can help if anyone ever uses your work without permission. Registration provides evidence of the validity of your copyright, so if you are ever in a legal dispute over who owns the material, you will be assumed to be the owner unless the other side can prove otherwise.

You can register your copyrighted material in the U.S. by sending completed forms, a $45 registration fee, and a copy of your work to the U.S. Copyright Office.

You'll need either Form TX or Short Form TX, depending on several different factors. The best way to get a copy of the right form for you is to visit the Copyright Office's website and follow the instructions at **www.copyright.gov/register/literary.html**. Otherwise, you can contact:

U.S. Copyright Office

Address: Library of Congress
              Copyright Office
              101 Independence Avenue, S.E.
              Washington, D.C. 20559-6000

Phone: (202) 707-3000

If you are Canadian, you can register a copyright for $50. Again, the easiest way to get information and a copy of the proper form is online. You can visit the Canadian Intellectual Property Office's site at **http://ic.gc.ca/sc_mrksv/cipo**. Enter the site then click on *Copyrights*. You can also reach the Intellectual Property Office at:

Canadian Intellectual Property Office

Address: Industry Canada
              Place du Portage I
              50 Victoria St., Room C-114
              Gatineau, Quebec K1A 0C9

Phone: (819) 997-1936

The information at the above websites is also useful if you want to learn more about copyrights covering other works, such as articles you write or tapes you produce.

> **NOTE:** When you register a copyright in your home country, it automatically protects your work in many countries around the world.

3.3.2   Using Material From Other Sources

It is usually okay to use small portions of copyrighted material as long as you give proper credit. The following scenario illustrates what I mean:

The Copyright Dinner Party

Imagine you have planned a dinner party for a group of people who will be arriving at your home in a few hours. To your dismay, you discover that you have no food in your refrigerator and no money to buy groceries. You see two possible solutions:

Solution 1

You climb through your neighbor's window and "borrow" a tofu steak you find in the fridge. You cook the steak for your dinner party and let your guests think you bought it especially for the occasion.

Solution 2

You climb through your neighbor's window and see the tofu steak, but you borrow just a few cubes. Next you go to the home of another neighbor and borrow some carrots. Then you borrow some green beans from the neighbor across the street, some corn from the neighbor at the end of the block, and some sprouts from a truck driver passing through town. In your search through the neighborhood you find an assortment of other vegetables and borrow a few of each.

You then rush home and mix all of the ingredients together, add some herbs from your own garden and some water to make a broth, and create a delicious stew using your own original recipe. As you serve the guests the stew you tell them where every one of the ingredients came from.

Solution 1 is a lot easier. Unfortunately, it is also illegal unless the owner has given you permission to do it. It is not okay to "borrow" a large portion of someone else's book, tape, speech, or other copyrighted material without permission – even if you give credit.

Solution 2 is usually acceptable. I say *usually* because, unfortunately, the law does not clearly define the exact number of words or lines that can be used without permission from the copyright owner. It is determined on a case-by-case basis.

> **NOTE:** It is okay to freely use material for which the copyright has expired. Most copyrights last for the life of the author

plus 70 years (50 years in Canada), so you can quote from Shakespeare's plays or other works for which copyright no longer exists.

If you are in doubt about whether you can use material from another source, it is a good idea to ask for permission. If you want to use material from a book, check the front of the book for the publishing company's contact information. Even if the copyright belongs to the author rather than the publisher, you would contact the "Permissions Officer" at the publishing house to request permission to use the material. It is a good idea to phone or e-mail if you need an answer quickly.

4. Speaking Skills

4.1 Traits of a Good Speaker

For over 10 years I have taught public speaking to adult students at the University of Calgary. At the end of every semester, each student gives a speech and is evaluated by classmates. Some of the students do a tremendous amount of research for their speeches. Others focus less on the research and more on their delivery. Over the years the students have been consistent in their evaluation. They have a clear preference when it comes to which types of speakers they prefer.

So, who do you think rates higher?

(a) A speaker with fabulous information and so-so delivery

(b) A speaker with fabulous delivery and so-so information

The answer is (b). Of course, the ideal situation is to have both fabulous information and fabulous delivery. However, for many audiences, your delivery is the most critical factor and it can make a significant difference in how the information is perceived. Poor delivery can make the most interesting topic sound boring, while excellent delivery can make even a dull topic come alive.

This doesn't necessarily apply to famous speakers. People who came to hear Mother Teresa or Princess Diana talk were probably not too concerned with their speaking skills.

However, for those of us who are not as famous, our presentation skills definitely matter. Here are four traits of successful speakers. Following in section 4.2 are a number of different ways you can develop these traits.

Confidence

A basic trait professional speakers have is confidence. Good speakers may sometimes feel nervous, but they don't let it show. (And they never tell the audience they feel nervous!) Confidence is often judged on the basis of non-verbal factors. Speakers look and sound more confident when they make eye contact with the audience, move naturally, use audiovisual equipment effectively, and speak fluently (avoiding too many "uhs" and "ums").

While many speakers are confident, speakers who are outstanding are also:

- Credible
- Dynamic
- Natural

Credibility

Credibility is an audience's perception of how believable a speaker is. To be credible, a speaker must be seen as someone who is an expert on the topic. However, this does not mean someone who is a "know-it-all." As well as being knowledgeable, a credible speaker is likeable and trustworthy. An example of a speaker famous for having high credibility is Brian Tracy, who you can read about at **www.briantracy.com**.

Dynamism

Dynamic speakers are enthusiastic about their topic, and they share that enthusiasm with their audience through variety and energy in their voice, gestures, and body movements. Other terms that can be applied to these speakers are "high energy" and "passionate."

A famous example of a dynamic speaker is Anthony Robbins. You can read about him at **www.anthonyrobbins.com**.

Naturalness

Natural speakers don't lecture. Even when speaking in front of an audience of thousands, they speak as if they were having a conversation with a group of friends. Other terms that may be applied to these speakers are "real" or "down-to-earth." An example of a famous speaker with a natural style is Jack Canfield, who you can read about at **www. jackcanfield.com**.

Most excellent speakers (including the three speakers mentioned above, of course), have all of these traits.

4.2 How to Improve Your Skills

There are a number of ways to enhance the traits described above, and improve your speaking skills.

4.2.1 Get Speaking Engagements

As with any skill, one of the best ways to improve is by just doing it. With speaking, this means getting yourself in front of as many audiences as possible.

You could begin by assembling a group of friends to present your talk to, however, at some point you will need to practice in front of a "real" audience. Two excellent ways to do this are by getting free speaking engagements (covered in section 6.5.6) and by putting on your own seminars (covered in section 9.5).

4.2.2   Ask for and Use Feedback

While simply getting practice speaking in front of audiences can help you become a more confident speaker, you should also use these occasions as an opportunity to get feedback.

An easy way for audience members to give you feedback is by filling out evaluation forms. I have been distributing evaluation forms since I first started speaking. As a beginner, even with what I hoped was a natural and dynamic presentation style, I had an approval rating of about 3.5 out of 5.

The lower ratings stung, but I took all feedback to heart and incorporated audience suggestions into future speeches. Now my ratings are consistently above 4.5 out of 5, and sometimes reach 5 out of 5. (Incidentally, getting a 5 out of 5 may be a result of having a kind and generous audience rather than a reflection of speaking skills. Even outstanding speakers have room for improvement.)

On the facing page is an example of a speaker evaluation form that you can give to your audience to get feedback and ratings in a number of different areas. (Of course, you can ask about any areas you want feedback on.) You will get more honest feedback if the people filling out the forms remain anonymous.

4.2.3   Record Yourself

By recording your presentations, you can see or hear for yourself the areas where you may need to improve. You can find information on how to record yourself in section 6.4.

4.2.4   Take a Course

There are a variety of seminars and classes that can help you to improve your speaking skills. Prices range from less than $100 for a continuing education course to thousands of dollars for an intense seminar aimed at professional speakers.

Sample Speaker Evaluation Form

Speaker's Name: _____

Title of Speech: _____

Date: _____

Please rate the speaker's performance in the following areas on a scale of 1 (poor) to 5 (excellent)

	Poor			Excellent

Delivery:

Rate of speech (too fast, too slow, just right)	1	2	3	4	5
Volume (too loud, too quiet, just right)	1	2	3	4	5
Enthusiasm	1	2	3	4	5
Eye contact with audience	1	2	3	4	5
Appropriate gestures/facial expressions	1	2	3	4	5
Personal connection made with audience	1	2	3	4	5

Content:

Clear central idea	1	2	3	4	5
Speech contained useful information	1	2	3	4	5
Speech was free of irrelevant information	1	2	3	4	5
Speaker avoided using technical terms	1	2	3	4	5

Organization:

Introduction created interest in the topic	1	2	3	4	5
Speech was logical; easy to follow	1	2	3	4	5
Main idea(s) were clearly communicated	1	2	3	4	5
Sufficient information included to support points	1	2	3	4	5
Visual aids were used effectively	1	2	3	4	5

General Comments:

1. What did you find most useful about this program? Least useful?

2. What else would you like to see included in this program?

3. What was your overall impression of the speaker?

Continuing education programs in speaking and presentation skills are offered by many universities, colleges, and other continuing education providers. These programs may range from intensive two-day seminars to courses held several hours a week over an entire semester.

Check the Yellow Pages for local colleges and universities. If you can't find a listing for "continuing education," call the school's main switchboard. (You can also find information about locating continuing education programs in section 7.5 of this guide.)

Another place to learn speaking skills is through Dale Carnegie Training. Check your phone book for a local office, or search for a location and courses near you at **www.dalecarnegie.com.**

The National Speakers Association (NSA) and Canadian Association of Professional Speakers (CAPS) offer a variety of events to help improve speaking skills. You can find out about upcoming events and search for a local chapter at their websites.

Or you can find out about both organizations by calling or writing them:

National Speakers Association

Address:	1500 S. Priest Drive Tempe, AZ 85281
Phone:	(480) 968-2552
Website:	**www.nsaspeaker.org**

Canadian Association of Professional Speakers

Address:	1370 Don Mills Road Suite 300 Toronto, Ontario M3B 3N7
Phone:	(416) 847-3355
Website:	**www.canadianspeakers.org**

More information about NSA, CAPS, and other organizations for speakers around the world is included in the resource section of this guide.

The top training program for professional speakers is the Bill Gove Speech Workshop (BGSW). Known around the world as the Harvard of Professional Public Speaking Schools, since 1947 BGSW has trained many of the world's highest paid speakers including Zig Ziglar, Mark Victor Hansen, and many more.

It covers: how to deliver a speech worth $5,000 - $10,000 per hour, how to write your speech like the pros, how to persuade an audience to buy your products, how to add humor and excitement to your speeches, and much more. Visit **www.speechworkshop.com** for information.

4.2.5   Consider Joining Toastmasters

Toastmasters is an international non-profit organization that helps people develop speaking skills. As a beginning speaker, Toastmasters can help you develop confidence, credibility, and dynamism.

Toastmasters clubs usually meet for an hour per week, and provide the opportunity to practice speaking. Each member also receives manuals, a monthly magazine, and other resources on how to speak.

To find a chapter near you, you can check your local phone book, visit the Toastmasters website at **www.toastmasters.org**, or call their world headquarters in California at (949) 858-8255.

If you decide to join, there is a $20 new member fee, plus dues of $27 every six months. Local Toastmasters clubs may also charge small fees to cover their expenses.

4.2.6   Work With a Coach

Working one-on-one with a coach can be very helpful in developing your presentation skills. Some coaches also provide a variety of other services such as assisting with speechwriting, image consulting, and marketing advice. Prices may start at $50 per hour and range up to thousands of dollars.

You can find speech coaches by networking with other speakers, and some coaches are listed in section 9.3.4 of this book.

4.2.7   Read Articles and Books About Speaking

The Internet is a great place to find articles on improving your skills. Many speaking coaches (see section 9.3.4) publish helpful tips at their websites. Some other useful online resources include:

- *Presentations.com*
  (Click on "Presentations" then on "Delivery")
  www.presentations.com

- *Presentations with Punch*
  http://members.shaw.ca/toasted/new_page_2.htm

- *Presenters Online – Presentation Tips*
  www.presentersonline.com/tutorials

There are also many excellent books available to help you develop your speaking skills. You can find books on speaking at the library, in a bookstore, or online. Here are a few you may find especially helpful:

- *10 Days to More Confident Public Speaking*, by The Princeton Language Institute and Lenny Laskowski

- *Knockout Presentations: How to Deliver Your Message with Power, Punch and Pizzazz*, by Diane Diresta

- *Inspire Any Audience*, by Tony Jeary

- *Secrets of Successful Speakers*: *How You Can Motivate, Captivate and Persuade*, by Lilly Walters

- *Speaking Secrets of the Masters*, by Terrence J. McCann

- *Success Secrets of the Motivational Superstars: America's Greatest Speakers Reveal Their Secrets*, by Michael Jeffreys

5. Setting Up a Speaking Business

If you work full-time delivering speeches for one company, you may not need to worry about setting up your own business. However, most speakers are self-employed, so setting up a business can help to manage your career and your income.

5.1 Getting Started

Before we get into the details of what needs to be done to run a successful speaking business, you'll find some basic information about starting any type of business. First, here are some good resources for starting a business:

SCORE

The Service Corps of Retired Executives has volunteers throughout the U.S. who donate time to mentor small businesses free of charge. Visit their website at **www.score.org** for helpful information or call (800) 634-0245 to find the nearest SCORE counseling location.

Small Business Administration

The SBA is an excellent source of free information for anyone starting a business in the U.S. To learn about SBA programs and services, call the SBA Small Business Answer Desk at (800) U-ASK-SBA (1-800-827-5722) or visit their website at **www.sba.gov**.

U.S. Chamber of Commerce

The U.S. Chamber of Commerce website offers free information on preparing a business plan, incorporating, choosing your office location, and other aspects of starting and running a business. Phone 1-800-638-6582 or visit their website at **www.uschamber.com/sb/learn/startup.htm**.

Online Small Business Workshop

The Canadian government offers a website dedicated to the needs of entrepreneurs, which includes an Online Small Business Workshop with information about taxes, financing, incorporation, and other topics. The website is located at **www.canadabusiness.ca**.

Nolo.com Small Business Legal Encyclopedia

Nolo is a publisher of plain English legal information, books, software, forms, and a comprehensive website. Their website also offers free advice on a variety of other small business matters in addition to legal issues. Visit **www.nolo.com**.

5.1.1 Choosing a Company Name

To choose a name for your company, start by taking a look at the types of names other speaking businesses have chosen. A quick and easy way to find this information is through the Internet. A great place to find company names is at the National Speakers Association site (**www. nsaspeaker.org/CVWEB_NSA/default.asp**).

Many speakers choose a name that has the following characteristics:

- is memorable

- incorporates their name

- reflects what they do

- will appeal to the particular audience they have targeted

For example, I used You're It Communications for my business name when I started presenting communications programs because my name is Tag (it's easy to remember "Tag, You're It"). The name also emphasized the service I performed for my clients (as in *"You're* it").

For good advice on what to consider when choosing a business name, visit **www.nolo.com**. (Click on "Business & Human Resources," then "Starting a Business," then "Naming Your Business.") You can also find helpful advice for choosing both a business name and tag line at **www.yudkin.com/generate.htm**. A tag line is a saying that accompanies your business name. For example, one of the tag lines used by FabJob is "Got a drab job? Get a FabJob!"

In most jurisdictions, if you operate under anything other than your own name, you are required to file for a fictitious name. It's usually just a short form to fill out and a small filing fee that you pay to your state or provincial government. Before registering a fictitious name, you will need to make sure it does not belong to anyone else. If someone else has trademarked the name you are using, you may be forced to stop using the name and possibly have to pay the owner damages.

To determine whether a name has already been registered, you can start by searching the federal trademark database with the U.S. Patent and Trademark Office (PTO) at **www.uspto.gov/main/trademarks.htm**. Canadians can find information and search an online database of existing trademarks through the Canadian Intellectual Property Office at **http://patents1.ic.gc.ca/intro-e.html.**

Most small businesses do not bother to trademark their names because it can be costly and time-consuming. However, if your company name is truly unique, you might want to consider it. If you do not have legal training, you can hire a lawyer specializing in "intellectual property."

5.1.2   Legal Matters

Your Business Legal Structure

Your business structure affects the cost of starting your business, your taxes, and your liability (responsibility) for any debts of the business. There are several different legal forms a business can have.

Sole Proprietorship

If you want to run the business yourself, without incorporating, your business will be known as a "sole proprietorship." This is the least expensive way to start a business. It is also the easiest because it requires less paperwork and you can report your business income on your personal tax return. One drawback to this type of business is that you are personally liable for any debts of the business.

Partnership

If you want to go into business with someone else, the easiest and least expensive way to do this is by forming a partnership. Legally, you would both be responsible for any debts of the company.

Corporation

Whether you are working alone or with partners, if you want a more formal legal structure for your business, you can incorporate. Incorporation can protect you from personal liability and may make your business appear more professional to some clients. However, it usually costs several hundred dollars and there are many rules and regulations involved with this type of business structure (among other requirements, corporations must file articles of incorporation, hold regular meetings, and keep records of those meetings). Many new business owners consult with an attorney before incorporating.

Limited Liability Company

A limited liability company is a new type of business legal structure in the U.S. It is a combination of a partnership and corporation, and is considered to have some of the best attributes of both, including limited personal liability.

Working with a Partner

Beyond any legal issues, before going into business with a partner you should spend many hours talking about how you will work together, including:

- What each of you will be responsible for

- How you will make decisions on a day-to-day basis

- What percentage of the business each of you will own

- How you see the business developing in the future

- What you expect from each other

During your discussions you can learn if there are areas where you need to compromise. For example, you may want the business to exist in order to promote yourself as a speaker, while your partner may want to eventually turn the company into a speaker's bureau. You can avoid future misunderstandings by putting the points you have agreed on into a written "partnership agreement" that covers any possibility you can think of (including one of you leaving the business in the future).

The resources at the start of this chapter have further information on business structures. Excellent advice is also offered at the Quicken website at **www.quicken.com/small_business/start**.

Business Licenses

You can find information about getting a city business license from your city hall. Depending on the nature of your business, you may also need to register with your county, state, or province.

For example, in the province of British Columbia, companies may need to register with the Private Post-Secondary Education Commission to present seminars to the public. So be sure to check with regulatory agencies in your area. Check the resources mentioned in the first part of this section or see the SBA's webpage at **www.sba.gov/hotlist/license.html**.

5.1.3   Setting Up Your Office

Location

The first thing you will need is a place to work. Your choices include working from home or renting space. Many speakers choose to work from home when they start their businesses, because it saves on the cost of an office.

Although clients may not come to your office, you will need to ensure you have enough space to carry out your business. Ask yourself if you will need space for other employees or for storing materials, and work from a place that offers you what you need.

Working from Home

There are many benefits to working from home. For example, you don't have to commute to an office, you can take breaks whenever you want, you can spend more time with your family, etc.

Another important benefit is that you are allowed to deduct from your income tax a percentage of your mortgage interest and property tax (or your rent) along with a similar share of some utilities and maintenance. See the section on taxes to find out where to get information and forms for business deductions.

If office space is expensive in your area and you have enough room to work from home, your financial breaks can really add up. Before you decide, however, be sure your local zoning laws allow you to have a home-based business in your neighborhood. Zoning laws are often regulated by a city or county's planning department. To contact the department, look up "zoning" or "planning" in the government section of your phone book.

To help you focus on business, and keep other family members from intruding on your workspace, try to find at least an entire room to use for your office. (Having a separate room also makes it easier to calculate your tax deduction.) You could work from a spare bedroom, a den, a basement, or any other area that can be kept separate from the rest of the house. Set regular office hours when the rest of the family knows you're working and not to be interrupted unless there's an emergency.

If you do choose to work from home, do not advertise that fact to potential employers. You will appear more successful if you have a "business" address. If your home address clearly sounds like a residential address, such as 1234 Hummingbird Estates Place, you may want to consider "renting" an address from a business like Mailboxes Etc., which offers a mail-forwarding service.

TIP: To avoid giving potential clients the impression that you are working out of your basement, do not use a PO Box as your address.

Renting Space

While a home office works well for many speakers, others prefer to rent a separate space. If you find it challenging to stay motivated, or tend to get easily distracted when you're at home, an office may be just what you need to help you focus on business.

A separate space also creates a better impression if you plan to have people visit. If you want a place to meet with clients or work with employees, you might want to consider getting an office outside your home.

Look for a place that is convenient to get to from your home, and that gives you quick access to any services you may need. Such services might include your bank, office supply stores, or even a good coffee shop! Pick an area that suits your needs and fits your budget.

For good advice on what to consider before renting space, check out the resources mentioned at the start of this chapter.

Telephones

You'll notice this section is titled "Telephones" rather than simply "Telephone." That's because many speakers have more than one phone. For many, the basics are: a business line, a fax line, and a cell phone.

If you are online a lot, emailing clients or doing research, and don't have access to a high speed cable connection, you may also want a separate line to connect to the Internet. If you have employees, you may want phone lines for them as well.

Here is some information to help you decide what is best for you – and how to best use the lines you have.

Your Business Line

A true business line will cost a little more than a residential line but you will be listed under your business name in the white pages, receive a listing in the Yellow Pages, and clients will be able to find you through directory assistance.

If you work at home, it's a good idea to have a separate telephone line that is off limits to the rest of the family. If a client's call is answered by a family member saying "Hello," you will probably be taken less seriously by the client. If a child answers your phone, you will almost certainly lose credibility in the eyes of the client. This kind of telephone answering can cost you more than a separate phone line would!

Your telephone should always be answered professionally with the name of your business. If you want to ensure your phone is answered at all times during business hours, you can hire someone to answer it for you.

> **TIP:** Do NOT hire an answering service that only takes messages. These are the type of services that say in response to callers' questions: "I don't know, I'm just the answering service." This is frustrating to callers and can create a poor impression.

If you decide to use someone to answer your calls, it is better to hire an individual, possibly working from home, who can answer callers' questions and act as a public relations person for you. See the information below for hiring employees.

A less expensive option to hiring someone to answer your calls is to use voice mail. Voice mail is widely accepted in business communication. If you do opt for voice mail, consider leaving your pager or cell phone number for callers who may have an urgent need to reach you.

Additional Phones

Even if your voice mail comes on while you're on the phone, it's wise to have a separate line for faxes. A potential client may not be impressed to hear you say, "Please wait a few minutes before sending that fax because I have to switch on the machine" (it suggests you are just a beginner working from home).

If there will be more than one person in the office or if you expect a moderate to heavy amount of incoming calls, you should consider buying a two-line phone and getting a roll-over line. Your local phone company can set up the service.

You should also get a cell phone as soon as possible. As a successful speaker, you can expect to spend a lot of time away from your office, especially when you're on the road at speaking engagements. Any time you are away from the office, you risk missing a call from someone who wants to hire you.

A cell phone enables you to check messages on your voice mail and return calls as soon as possible. You should be able to get a cell phone from the company that provides your business line or pick one up at your local shopping mall.

1-800 Numbers

You can get a 1-800 number through any telephone company. Whenever someone calls, you will pay for the call. As rates vary, shop around to find a company that will give you a low per-minute rate.

To help potential employers remember your number, ask if you can get a "vanity" number that spells out your company name or something that refers to your services. For example, my old number was 1-800-HEART-24 – a great number for a relationship speaker!

Equipment and Supplies

In addition to telephones, you will need a variety of office equipment and supplies for your business.

Check with your local office supply stores, such as Staples and Office Depot, to find out about sales. The sales reps who work there can also be of assistance when it comes to putting together everything you need for your office.

Computer and Software

If you don't already have a computer, you should consider buying or leasing one for your business as soon as you can afford it. In addition to the computer and printer, it's a good idea to get a flash drive or CD-RW (rewriteable CD drive) so you can back up your files.

Check with a computer consultant or computer specialist at an office products store for advice on the best products to protect your computer, such as a firewall, virus software, and surge protector.

Many computers already have the basic software needed to run a business. While Microsoft Office and other programs that came with your computer can be used in your business, you will also need a bookkeeping program such as Quicken or QuickBooks.

To keep track of clients, including contact information, you can use a database program that came with your computer (if you have MS Office, you could use MS Outlook) or you could buy a database program such as ACT! or FileMaker Pro.

Fax Machine and Photocopier

Both of these are optional. You may be able to use fax software that you have on your computer or go to the local copy shop when you need photocopies. If it will be more convenient to have them in your office, consider getting a combination fax-printer-scanner-copier unit.

File Cabinet

You'll need to organize and store information you receive, as well as keep files for each client. Your desk may have drawers that can hold files, but you will probably eventually need a file cabinet. Your options include two-door or four-door filing cabinets, or you may find a lateral file cabinet with a wood finish that fits beautifully with the rest of your office furniture.

Supplies

Of course you will need the supplies any business needs, including pens and pencils, paper, stapler, clips, Post-Its, scissors, tape, Liquid Paper or correction tape, etc.

Stationery

Your stationery should present a consistent image, and promote you as a successful speaker. In addition to the professional speaker materials described in section 6.3.2, you will need business cards, letterhead and envelopes.

Your stationery can help reassure prospective clients that you are a professional. Consider using heavy textured papers, raised printing, and a professional design. Some speakers use color business cards with their photograph and contact information on the front, and their services or benefits on the back. Check around for prices at print shops or office supply stores.

If your start-up finances are limited, you might want to consider getting business cards from VistaPrint.com. They offer color business cards on heavy paper stock, available with a number of different designs. You can get 250 cards for only $29.95 plus shipping. Visit **www.Vista Print.com** or call 1-800-721-6214.

Insurance

Once you have equipped your office, you should protect what you have. Having insurance could save your business one day. There are other types of insurance, and many different levels of coverage available for each type. An insurance broker (check the Yellow Pages) can advise you of your options and shop around for the best rates for you. Types of insurance include:

Property Insurance

Property insurance protects the contents of your business (e.g. your computer, any supplies, office furniture) in case of fire, theft, or other losses. If you have a home office, your business property may not be covered by your homeowner's policy.

Errors and Omissions

This type of insurance protects you in case you make a mistake or have a misunderstanding with a client.

Life and Disability Insurance

If you provide a portion of your family's income, then you need to carry life insurance and disability insurance to make certain they are cared for if something happens to you. If you become sick or otherwise disabled for an extended period, your business could be in jeopardy. Disability insurance would provide at least a portion of your income while you're not able to be working.

Car Insurance

Be sure to ask your broker about your auto insurance if you'll be using your personal vehicle on company business.

Health Insurance

If you live in the United States and aren't covered under a spouse's health plan, you'll need to consider your health insurance options. You can compare health insurance quotes at **www.ehealthinsurance.com** which offers plans from over 150 insurance companies nationwide.

> **TIP:** Some insurance companies offer discount pricing for members of particular organizations. When you are looking for organizations to join, whether your local Chamber of Commerce or a national association, check to see if discounted health insurance is one of the member benefits.

Canadians have most of their health care expenses covered by the Canadian government. For expenses that are not covered (such as dental care, eyeglasses, prescription drugs, etc.) self-employed professionals may get tax benefits from setting up their own private health care plan. Puhl Employee Benefits (**www.puhlemployeebenefits.com**) is an example of the type of financial planning company that can help you set up your own private health care plan.

More Information

The Small Business Administration has an excellent insurance and risk management guide for small businesses available online at **www.sba.gov/tools/resourcelibrary/publications/serv_pub_mplan.html** (scroll down to #17).

5.2 Finances

5.2.1 Start-Up Funding

The cost of starting your business might range from almost nothing to thousands of dollars. Obviously, your start-up expenses will be much higher if you decide to rent space, buy equipment, and get professional demo materials made (discussed in section 6.4).

You will also need to consider your "working capital" requirements. This is the money you will need for the day-to-day operation of your business. There are other expenses that will come out of your pocket before you get your first client, like business cards, telephone, etc.

Many speakers are optimistic about how much money they will earn from their business, and how quickly they will earn it. While you may be tremendously successful right from the start and exceed your own expectations, it is wise to be prepared for the possibility that it may take longer than expected until your business is earning enough to support you.

A standard rule of thumb is to have six months' worth of living expenses set aside beyond your start-up costs. Or you might consider remaining at your current job and working part-time on your speaking business until it is established.

Depending on the start-up costs you calculate, you may find you have all the money you need to get started in your savings account (or available to spend on your credit cards). If your own resources won't cover all the things you would like to do with your business, you will need to look for financing. One place to look for financing is from family members. They may be willing to invest in your company or give you a loan to help you get started. To avoid any misunderstandings, it's wise to get any agreements in writing even with family members.

If you decide to approach a bank for a business loan, be prepared. Write a loan proposal that includes detailed information about your business, how much money you want to borrow, what you plan to do with the money, and so on.

Some good advice about financing can be found at the SBA and Nolo sites given at the start of this chapter. Also look into the Small Business Administration business assistance programs. The SBA has a Loan Guarantee Program that provides loans to small businesses. Contact your local SBA office or go to **www.sba.gov**, then click on "Services" and choose "Financial Assistance."

5.2.2   Keeping Track of Your Money

There are a variety of resources available to help you keep track of your business income and expenses.

Financial Institution

The first of these resources is a financial institution – a bank, trust company, or credit union – where you will open your business checking account.

You can shop around to find a financial institution that is supportive of small business, or use the same one that you use for your personal banking. In addition to your checking account, a financial institution may provide you with a corporate credit card you can use to make purchases for your business.

Bookkeeping System

Your bookkeeping system is a record of your expenses and income. To keep track of your expenses, you will need to keep copies of all receipts. This can sometimes be a challenge for new business owners who might have a habit of tossing out receipts for small items (or not asking for receipts in the first place). However, you are likely to have numerous small expenses related to your business, and these can add up over time.

The cup of coffee you buy for a prospective client, the mileage you travel to a client's office, the pack of paper you pick up at the office supply store, the postage you pay when sending out information packets – these and many other expenses should be accounted for so you can minimize your taxes. And, of course, knowing exactly where your money is going will help you plan better and cut back on any unnecessary expenses. So make it a habit to ask for a receipt for every expense related to business.

If you have the time, you can do your own bookkeeping. As mentioned in the section on software, programs such as Quicken or QuickBooks can make the job much easier for you. These programs can also be used to prepare invoices. You can get good advice to help you with managing your finances and developing your business at **http://quicken.intuit.com**.

If you find yourself so busy with speaking engagements that you don't have time to do your own bookkeeping, consider hiring a part-time bookkeeper on a contract basis to do your bookkeeping for you. Depending on how busy you are, it may take the bookkeeper a few hours per week to get your books up to date and balance them with your bank statements. You can find a bookkeeper through word of mouth or check the Yellow Pages.

Financial Experts

You may want to hire experts to assist with your finances. An accountant or tax advisor can be expensive (e.g. you might pay $100 per hour compared to the $20 per hour you might pay a bookkeeper). However, their advice could possibly save you hundreds or even thousands of dollars at tax time.

If you're not able to find an accountant or tax advisor through word of mouth, you can try the Yellow Pages.

5.2.3   Taxes

If your business is a sole proprietorship or partnership in the United States, you will file a Schedule C form with your personal tax returns. You'll also have to file a form to determine the amount you owe on your social security.

If you file a U.S. tax return, you will need to include either your Social Security Number or an Employer Identification Number (EIN). A number of business owners recommend filling out an SS-4 Form to obtain an EIN even if your business is a sole proprietorship. Your corporate clients will need this for their records, as will suppliers if you want to sell products at your speeches. An EIN is also required if your company is incorporated or if you have employees.

You may also be required to pay taxes in the jurisdictions you speak in. For tax information, forms and publications, see the resources at the start of this chapter or contact your government's tax authority. Check your local phone directory for an office near you, call their national office, or visit their website.

The U.S. Internal Revenue Service (IRS) can be reached at 1-800-829-4933 or online at **www.irs.gov**. In Canada, you can get information from the Canada Revenue Agency at 1-800-959-5525 or online at **www.cra-arc. gc.ca/menu-e.html**.

5.2.4   Contracts

You should have a contract for every speaking engagement. A contract is a document signed by both you and the client which states what services you will provide, how much you will be paid, and other points you have agreed on. This is an important detail that must not be overlooked. Without a contract, you may not get paid!

If you get a speaking engagement through a speakers' bureau (see chapter 8), they should take care of the contract. Ultimately, however, it is still your responsibility to ensure at all times that you have a copy of a signed contract before you speak. As most of your early speaking engagements will probably not come through speakers' bureaus, it is up to you to produce your own contracts.

Getting Paid

One of the most important elements of a speaking contract is a clause specifying when you will be paid. As a speaker, you may ask to get paid in full on the day you speak. Or you could ask for half the speaking fee up front to hold the date, with a check for the balance at or before the speaking event. However, if you are presenting a series of programs to a corporation, they may have a standard policy of paying 30 days after you send them an invoice.

Following is a sample contract for a fictional speaker (Sam Speaker) to give you some ideas for your own contracts. You can use it as a starting point for creating your own documents, but of course you should review any contract with your attorney before using it.

Sample Contract

(ON COMPANY LETTERHEAD)

Speaking Program Contract

Client

Jane Jones
Human Resources Department
City of Sunnyday
123 Main Street
Sunnyday, CA 90211

Purpose

To deliver a keynote speech for the City of Sunnyday's Annual Employee Appreciation Day.

Details

Sam Speaker will present a keynote speech on the topic of "Work is Wonderful" on June 20, 2008 from 2:00 p.m. to 3:00 p.m. at the Civic Center in Sunnyday, California.

The client will be responsible for facility arrangements, audio-visual equipment, and duplicating printed materials for participants. Sam Speaker Services Ltd. will provide a master handout for duplication.

Fees

The fee is $1,500, plus tax and expenses. A deposit of $750 is required to confirm the booking, with the balance of $750 due 7 days before the event. Two invoices are enclosed. Expenses (airfare, ground transportation, hotel, meals, etc.) will be billed after the program.

...2

- 2 -

If the program is cancelled or postponed by the client for any reason, Sam Speaker Services shall be paid the appropriate postponement or cancellation charge as noted below:

Days Prior to Scheduled Program	Postponement/ Date Change	Cancellation of Program
30 - 90	10%	25%
11 - 29	25%	50%
10 or fewer	50%	100%

In the event the chosen speaker is unable to appear, Sam Speaker Services will send a suitable replacement. If a replacement speaker cannot be found, all fees paid will be refunded.

Signature and Date

Jane Jones	Sam Speaker
Human Resources Dept.	President
City of Sunnyday	Sam Speaker Services

Date	Date

Cancellation Clause

An important element of a speaking contract is a cancellation clause, or a statement that explains what will happen if a speaking event is cancelled or postponed.

For example, some speakers have a clause which says if the client cancels the engagement, for any reason, less than a certain number of days before the event (e.g. 30, 60, or 90 days), the client forfeits the deposit. If the event could possibly be postponed, you can also include a postponement charge.

Invoices

If you are presenting a series of programs for a client, you may need to provide an invoice in order to get paid.

Sample Invoice

(ON COMPANY LETTERHEAD)

Invoice

DATE: July 24, 2008

TO: Jane Jones
Human Resources Department
City of Sunnyday
123 Main Street
Sunnyday, CA 90211

RE: **City of Sunnyday Leadership Training Program**

Design of Communication Workshop	$1,500.00
July 22, 2008 Workshop Delivery	3,000.00
July 23, 2008 Workshop Delivery	3,000.00
Subtotal	7,500.00
7% Tax *(Include your own tax rate here)*	525.00
Total – Please pay this amount	**$8,025.00**

TERMS: Payable within 30 days.
Thank you for your business.

As you can see from the sample on the facing page, your invoice should be on your letterhead and include:

- The client name and contact information

- A purchase order number (if the client gave you one)

- A list of services you provided with the date and cost of each

- Any expenses and taxes payable

- The total amount due

- Terms of payment according to your contract (e.g. "Payable within 30 days")

5.3 Preparing for a Speech

You may have several tasks once a speech is booked. These may include:

- Making travel arrangements

- Deciding what audio-visual equipment you will need

- Keeping in touch with the event organizer

- Arranging for copying of materials

- Preparing audiovisuals

- Shipping any products to the event facility

- Arranging for staff to work at your products table

Some of the above items may be taken care of by the event organizer, such as booking your AV equipment and arranging for photocopying. However, you will need to discuss them with the organizer. The organizer can also give you the information you need to customize your speech, and let you know if you will be picked up at the airport.

In some cases, they may also make your travel arrangements. If you are responsible for your own arrangements (to be reimbursed later), you can find good details on travel through a travel agent or the Internet. Websites that allow you to compare rates include **Travelocity.com** and **Expedia.com**.

When it comes to getting staff to work at your products table (see section 9.2 for a discussion of products), you may be able to get volunteers from the organization you are speaking for, use your own staff (see below) or can contact a temporary agency in the city you will travel to. You can find temporary agencies in the Yellow Pages.

5.4 Employees and Contractors

You may be working on your own when you first start your business, but at some point you could decide to hire people to help you with a variety of duties, such as:

- marketing you to potential employers (described in section 6.3)

- answering the telephone

- helping with office duties

- handling bookkeeping

- acting as a personal assistant

Whenever you hire someone, you will either sign them on as employees or as contractors. What's the difference?

- You may train employees. Contractors are trained elsewhere.

- Employees work only for you. Contractors may have their own customers and work for other firms.

- Employees are paid on a regular basis. Contractors are paid per project.

- Employees work for a certain amount of hours, while contracted workers set their own hours, as long as they get the job done.

- Employees can be fired or quit. Contractors can't be fired in the usual way while they are working under contract. You may decide to have them stop working on a project, but you will be obliged to pay them according to your contractual agreement unless you are able to renegotiate the contract or successfully sue them if you are unhappy with their work. (Of course that would only be in extreme cases; it is best to avoid lawsuits altogether!)

As a speaker, if you hire individuals to provide services such as speechwriting or coaching, they will likely be self-employed contractors. However, the other people who work for your company may be either employees or contractors, and there are different tax requirements for each. For more information about employment taxes, check the tax resources listed in section 5.2.3.

Check the resources provided at the start of this chapter for excellent advice on hiring employees and contractors.

Before you hire, you should also check with your local department of labor to find out all the rules and regulations required as an employer. There may be other state and federal rules and regulations that may apply to you, including: health and safety regulations, Workers' Compensation, minimum wage and unemployment insurance.

6. Getting Hired

6.1 Who Hires Speakers?

Speakers are hired by a variety of employers (in this guide the term "employers" includes clients of self-employed speakers), including:

- Conference and trade show organizers

- Professional associations

- Local and national seminar companies

- Corporations of all types and sizes

- Government agencies

- Non-profit organizations

- Continuing education departments

- Schools

- Colleges

- Cruise ships

While some speakers do very well selling their services to only one type of employer, the vast majority of speakers work with several different types of employers to ensure a steady flow of income.

The bottom line: although one type of employer may be most appealing to you right now, it is highly recommended that you read through the information about each type of employer, because chances are you will end up working for more than one.

6.2 A Potential Employer's Greatest Fear

Knowing a potential employer's greatest fear can give you a huge advantage over your competition. With this information, you can show potential employers exactly why the thing they fear most will not happen if they hire you.

So what is it that people who employ speakers fear? I will illustrate with a personal example from a time I hired a speaker without seeing him speak or checking his references:

> I had hired a private investigator to speak on the topic of "Con Men and Gold Diggers" at a singles conference on relationship issues. I cringed when the first words out of the speaker's mouth were: "There's a con man or a gold digger in this room. They come to events like this." But it got worse.

> Minutes into his talk he suddenly noticed a beautiful blonde in her early twenties in the audience. He stopped mid-sentence. "What are you doing here?" he asked the young woman, singling her out in front of the group. "You certainly don't need to attend something like this." The implication, of course, was that not only had she made a mistake in attending, but that the rest of the conference registrants were losers who "needed" to attend a singles conference.

> As he continued speaking, he stopped occasionally to insult or make inappropriate comments to audience members. He picked on several of the men and told a woman in her fifties that "a handsome woman like you should have no problem finding a man."

Meanwhile, my partner Clayton and I were frantically conferring at the back of the room about what to do. The man was supposed to talk for an hour! We couldn't allow it to continue. About 20 minutes into his talk we said we were running behind and would have to cut his talk short.

To our amazement, about half the people in the audience protested. They were enjoying his talk! "You said I had an hour!" he complained, not moving from the front of the room. "Shorten the wine and cheese reception instead," an audience member yelled. We ended up letting him speak for the full hour and, of course, heard complaints afterwards from those who felt the same way as we did about the talk.

What we experienced is one of the worst nightmares of anyone who hires speakers – a speaker who insults the audience. (By the way, a speaker doesn't have to pick on individual audience members to be insulting. The same result can be achieved by making statements that are racist, sexist, or otherwise demeaning to a group.)

When a speaker messes up, the person who looks bad is the person who hired the speaker. Bad speakers can go on with life without ever again having to face the audience members they disappointed. The person who hired the speaker doesn't get off so easily. She may have to face her boss, co-workers, professional colleagues, or other important people. These people will probably question her judgment and may lose trust in her abilities.

Hiring a speaker who insults the audience can definitely be damaging to the career of the person who hired the speaker! But it's not only the insulting speaker who can make the person who did the hiring look bad. Among the other types of speakers feared by employers are:

- The boring speaker

- The speaker who has nothing new to say

- The speaker who acts like they know it all and "talks down" to the audience

- The speaker who knows so little about the topic they can't answer basic questions from the audience

- The speaker who uses a high tech presentation that doesn't work properly

- The speaker who speaks so softly they can't be heard

- The speaker who gets flustered or upset by simple challenges like a light bulb burning out on a projector

- The drunk speaker

- The speaker who delivers a sales pitch for something the audience is not interested in

- The speaker whose comments or approach are inappropriate for the audience

EXAMPLE:
I remember sitting through an embarrassing business seminar where a speaker tried to get an audience of senior lawyers to do silly things like writing cute sayings on their nametags, such as "Jolly John" or "Marvelous Marvin." It was several years before that organization decided to hire another speaker.

"But I'm nothing like that!" you may be thinking. The point is: potential employers fear you may be the type of speaker who will make them look bad, unless you give them solid evidence to the contrary.

In this section you will discover a number of techniques to show potential employers that you are a true professional, and to allay any fears they may have about hiring you. Communicate like a pro, and not only will you be more likely to get the job, but the person who hires you will sleep easier at night.

6.3 How to Approach Potential Employers

The first thing to know when you are approaching people about speaking opportunities is that there is no single method to use with all potential employers. This section offers an overview of several different ways that successful speakers use to approach potential employers. The sections in chapter 7 have more detail about what usually works best with specific types of employers, and in section 6.5 you will find some great ideas on how to get potential employers to approach you.

6.3.1   Calling Potential Employers

You may be the type of person who hates to get sales calls from people you don't know. However, the "cold call" (a sales call to a stranger) works in many selling situations. If it didn't, you would never have your dinner interrupted by people trying to sell you carpet cleaning.

The difference between you and the person who sells carpet cleaning is that you will be contacting people whose job it is to answer calls like yours. Armed with all the benefits you have to offer this prospective employer, you should see your call as simply an introduction of your services – services that can help this person and organization.

Getting Through to the Right Person

The first things you will need to make your calls successful are names and phone numbers of prospective employers. Chapter 7 explains where you can get this information for many different types of employers.

The person who can make the decision to hire you, or "the decision-maker," is the ideal person for you to speak with. So, what if you have a company name, but not a name or phone number for a decision-maker?

Ask the Receptionist for the Decision-Maker's Name

If you were calling a seminar company, for example, you would simply ask the receptionist, "Can you tell me the name of the person who hires speakers?" In many companies, the receptionist will either tell you the person's name or put you through to an assistant in the decision-maker's department.

Ask for the Decision-Maker's Direct Phone Line

Once you have the decision-maker's name, you can then ask what that person's direct phone number is. (Don't ask for the phone number before the name. You don't want to be asking, "What was your name?" if you do get through to the decision-maker.) If the receptionist says they can't give out that information, simply ask to be put through to the decision-maker's line.

You may possibly be able to find the decision-maker's direct line if you call back after business hours and get a voice mail system with a company directory. However, in many cases you won't need a direct line if the receptionist is willing to put your call through.

Deal With the Decision-Maker's Assistant

If the receptionist puts you through to an assistant in the decision-maker's department, you can go through the same procedure of asking for the decision-maker's name and direct phone number.

Be prepared, however, that the assistant may be a "gatekeeper." In other words, it may be the assistant's job to screen out calls from anyone the decision-maker doesn't know. While this doesn't happen nearly as often to speakers as it does to people breaking into another fab job, it is something to be prepared for.

If the assistant says "Just send us your information," politely explain that you would be happy to do that, but you want to ensure you send the information they need. Do not try to bully the assistant into putting you through. This person has the power in your relationship, and will not want to help someone who is rude. Instead, try asking the assistant for advice about the best way to reach the decision-maker.

The sections that follow this one offer some suggested alternatives in the event that you are not able to get through to the decision-maker on the telephone. However, let's assume that you will be put through to the decision-maker. Now you need to know what to say. Don't be surprised when you do get through to the decision-maker—after all, that is what happens to many speakers in many situations. Remember, you are contacting people whose job it is to find good speakers like you.

What to Say

It would be great if you could just strike up a spontaneous conversation with a prospective employer and get the job. However, most people who are starting out don't find it easy to say the right things off the top of their head. This is when having a script can be a tremendous help. A script is simply an outline of what you want to say during your call. It helps you clearly communicate the main points you want to get across.

What you will say in your script depends primarily on the goal you want to achieve. Do you want to arrange a meeting? Do you want to invite the potential employer to come and see you speak? Or do you simply want someone to return your call?

It's a good idea to have scripts for leaving a message on voice mail as well as for your first conversation with a potential employer. Be prepared for the fact that many decision-makers screen their calls with voice mail. They simply don't have time to speak with everyone who wants their attention. Whether or not they return your call depends primarily on how intriguing your message is.

Superstar speaker Mark Victor Hansen reports that when he used to call prospective employers he would leave a message simply stating his name, phone number, and the message, "It's good news." In many cases he found his message was intriguing enough to get people to call back. When a prospective employer returned the call, his "good news" was that he was available to work for them.

Mark Victor Hansen could get away with this because he is an incredibly charming man. It could work for you, too. However, many speakers find a more direct approach works best. That approach is to briefly and clearly offer something that a prospective employer wants.

If you worked for a corporation, would you return this call?

> *Um, hi. My name is Pat Talker. I'm a professional speaker. Well, actually, I'm just beginning my speaking career, but everyone tells me I'm really good. I sure hope you'll give me a chance. I'm very interesting. People also think I'm quite funny. I have some great stories and jokes I like to tell. I've done some volunteer speaking to different groups and all of them really liked me. A couple of groups even gave me a standing ovation.*

> *The thing I like speaking about most is customer satisfaction. I worked in customer service positions for years, and customers always said how happy they were with me. There was one time I...*

By now – in fact, long before now – most decision-makers would have deleted the message.

Compare that message to this one:

> *Hello (first and last name of potential employer), this is Pat Talker. I offer a program that helps companies improve customer satisfaction. Please give me a call at 555-1234 so we can discuss how this program would benefit (insert name of potential employer's company).*

If the company is looking to improve customer satisfaction – as many companies are – the second call is likely to get returned. I have made many such "pitch" calls to propose something I thought would interest the person I was calling, and many of those calls were returned.

By the way, there is probably no surefire way to get 100 percent of your calls returned unless you are Julia Roberts or you are calling from the IRS. (Of course you don't want to pretend to be someone you're not unless you want to face an angry employer!)

> **TIP:** You are much more likely to get your call returned if you can say you were referred by someone the decision-maker knows and respects. Ask for referrals after all your talks and slip "_____ suggested I call you" into your script right after your name.

Mistakes to Avoid

In the first example, the caller made several mistakes:

Saying "I'm Just a Beginner"

I can't think of an instance where you would want to volunteer the fact that you are a beginner. After all, how would you feel about your brain surgeon if he said he was "just a beginner?" It doesn't exactly instill confidence, does it? I suggest you stop seeing yourself as "just a beginner." See yourself instead as someone with plenty of value to offer potential employers.

Talking About "Me, Me, Me"

Notice how many times the caller said "I" or "me." Potential employers, like most other humans, are more interested in their own needs than hearing "me-focused" comments like these.

Telling, Not Showing

You are probably wasting your breath telling people you are "interesting," "funny," or have other wonderful traits. These are the sorts of things people usually need to see for themselves. Some of the other techniques described later, such as sending a video or inviting someone to hear you speak, will "show" rather than "tell" people that you are an excellent speaker.

Saying "I Hope You'll Give Me a Chance"

This statement sounds needy. It is definitely a major turn-off to many employers. The attitude to have when you make your calls is not that you are looking for someone to do you a favor. Instead, see yourself as a business person exploring whether doing business with this company would be beneficial for both of you.

The second example above works because it speaks in terms of the decision-maker's needs. Of course, your call should never sound like you are reading a script. Before you call, practice giving your pitch until it sounds completely natural.

"Why should I practice anything?" you may be thinking. "Why not just call and leave my name and phone number without a message?" Because many professional people will not return such a call. In my experience, most of the strangers who have left messages, and asked me to call them back without explaining why, have turned out to be people trying to sell me something I didn't want.

So communicate your message with confidence. Assume that what you offer is something the decision-maker wants. Your call is much more likely to be returned.

How Often Should You Call?

I have heard a few employers say that persistence pays off. In other words, someone who calls repeatedly will eventually get their call returned. However, they are probably the exception to the rule. Most employers say they are turned off by someone who "pesters" them. One woman told me she makes a mental note of the people who call repeatedly and resolves never to have anything to do with them.

Calling without leaving a message may seem like a good idea, but many business people have caller ID on their telephone. If they see a dozen calls from someone who doesn't leave a message, they are likely to assume the caller is selling something they would not be interested in. Not only will the decision-maker not pick up the phone, but they may become so irritated with the calls that they may respond negatively when the caller finally does leave a message.

If your first call is not returned, I recommend calling a second time a few days later, just in case your first message didn't get through. Messages are rarely erased accidentally, but you wouldn't want to miss a business opportunity if, for some reason, it happened to your call.

If neither of your calls are returned, it may be wise to wait awhile before calling again or focus instead on prospective employers who are interested in working with you.

Once You Get Through to the Decision-Maker

Many of the same principles for leaving a message apply when you are speaking directly with the decision-maker. For these calls, you should prepare and practice a script that works well for you. The following is the type of script I have found most effective. If the person answers the phone, I assume they are willing to talk, so I launch right into my script:

YOU: Hello (first name of potential employer), this is Pat Talker. I'm calling about a program that helps companies improve customer satisfaction.

TIP: Unless you have already met the person you are calling, avoid starting your conversation with pleasantries like "How are you today?" before stating your name and why you are calling. Using pleasantries with a stranger is often associated with people calling to "sell" something and may create suspicion.

YOU: *(Say lightly, as if the answer is obviously "yes")* I'm sure you would say customer satisfaction is something (insert name of potential employer's company) cares about, wouldn't you?

TIP: The decision-maker will respond at this point. Most should respond positively. If someone doesn't respond positively, you may want to cut the call short and move on to the next name on your list. Trying to turn someone around who won't respond politely to even the most basic question is almost always a waste of time and energy.

YOU: I thought so. My program can help (insert name of company) increase customer satisfaction and create more repeat business. I have a 15-minute presentation that explains the program in detail. I'd like to meet with you to go over it. Do you have 15 minutes in your schedule on Wednesday afternoon, or might Thursday morning work better for you?

As the example above illustrates, you can avoid a mistake many cold callers make of giving the decision-maker a choice between saying "yes" to a meeting or saying "no." Instead, give them a choice between two possible meeting dates. If you want to set up a meeting, you should also clearly state a time limit—ideally no more than 20 minutes—because many decision-makers view their time as limited.

At this point, don't be surprised to get at least a mild objection. An excellent way to respond is to agree with how the decision-maker feels and explain that many other people felt exactly the same way until they had a chance to learn more about your program. For example:

THEM: We don't have a need for this type of program right now.

YOU: I understand how you feel. Many of my clients felt exactly the same way until I was able to show them how they could benefit from this program. I'd like to show you the same thing. Would Wednesday afternoon work for you, or would Thursday morning be better?

If the decision-maker is still not interested, then move on to the next person on your list. If you are overly aggressive, most decision-makers will be turned off and may not want to do business with you even if they hear good things about you from another source. Your time could be better spent focusing on people who are interested in what you have to offer.

Don't worry if your first few calls don't go as planned. Consider them practice. Once you have been using this approach for a while, it should generate a respectable success rate. Depending on what you are proposing, a good success rate may be one "yes" out of every ten calls or even one "yes" out of every two calls. It is up to you to determine if making a lot of calls is a good use of your time.

If this approach doesn't work, you need to go back and take a hard look at your script. Are you clearly communicating the benefits of taking the action you suggest to the decision-maker? If you believe you are, ask someone you respect to listen to you making some of your calls. They may discover something in the way you communicate that could be improved.

Having Someone Phone for You

An alternative to phoning yourself is to have someone phone for you. This can give the impression that you are already an established speaker. Like many of us, employers can be influenced by how things appear, and may assume you must be a successful professional to have people working for you.

One way to have someone call for you is to hire someone you pay on an hourly or commission basis. This employee—a person sometimes referred to as "an agent"—might work for you full-time or part-time, from your office or from their home. You might find them through word of mouth or from a classified ad. In addition to phoning, you might have them assist you with other tasks, as well. You can find out more about hiring employees or contractors in chapter 5, "Setting Up a Speaking Business."

Another alternative is to have a friend or relative call on your behalf. Ideally this person should have a different last name from yours, or they should simply introduce themselves by first name. (It doesn't sound nearly as impressive to hear, "Hello, this is John Reynolds calling on behalf of Jane Reynolds.")

6.3.2   Preparing an Information Package

Another option is to prepare a letter or an information package and send it to potential employers. You could send this promotional material by regular mail or courier, or in the case of a letter, by fax or e-mail, then wait for your phone to ring...

...but you might be waiting a long time.

I know one highly paid speaker who spent $1,200 printing and mailing a beautiful color brochure to hundreds of prospects. She didn't receive a single response. With results like that, it's no wonder some people are happy with a one percent response rate.

It isn't just the speakers who have problems. The people who hire speakers sometimes complain that they are flooded with unsolicited promotional material. One speakers bureau owner has a basement filled with hundreds of unopened packages from speakers.

So why on earth would any speaker bother to send out information? The reason is because many potential employers will expect to see your materials before they hire you.

Most successful professional speakers have information packages. When a prospective employer asks for more information, these speakers generally do not send a few photocopied pages. Instead, they send something that is visually attractive and packed with information aimed at persuading the employer to hire them.

Following are some of the elements of an effective information package, which will be described in more detail below:

- folder

- cover letter

- business card

- resume or curriculum vitae

- biography

- color photograph

- one-sheets

- testimonial letters

- client list

- newspaper and magazine clippings

- brochures

- promotional items

The Folder

Your folder should preferably have two pockets so you can easily include everything in your information package.

Many successful professional speakers have folders printed in color with their name and photograph. If you are interested in doing the same, you can contact local printers for information and price quotes. If you shop around, you may be able to get personalized folders for as little as one dollar each for several hundred folders (although the price will depend on how many you order, how many colors you want, etc.). One company that specializes in printing folders is Presentation Folder, Inc. You can visit **www.presentationfolder.com** or call them at 1-800-927-1127.

If you are working with a limited budget, an inexpensive alternative is to buy some glossy two-color folders from a local stationer. For example, Staples offers a package of ten "twin-pocket laminated portfolios" for under $10. You could then personalize it by gluing your business card on the cover.

Your Cover Letter

Your cover letter, printed on attractive stationery to match your folder, should focus on the benefits you offer to the prospective employer. (Benefits are covered in section 2.5 of this guide.)

As was explained above, your cover letter should be personalized with the prospective employer's name. Double-check the spelling and avoid saying "Dear Mr." or "Dear Ms." unless you are certain of the gender of the person you are sending it to. I have received letters addressed to "Mr. Goulet" from people who assume that "Tag" is a man's name. (Tag is actually short for Therese Antoinette Goulet.) When in doubt, drop the salutation. Instead, you can include an "attention" line, like "Attention: Pat Reynolds."

Resume, Curriculum Vitae, and Biography

Each of these documents provides a summary of your background. In most cases, you would submit a resume and a biography. In a few circumstances, such as if you are applying to teach at a university, you may be asked for a *curriculum vitae*, also known as a CV.

Resume

A resume is a brief summary of your experience, education, and skills. Two pages is usually the recommended maximum for a resume.

When it comes to writing a resume, I recommend you be selective. Tailor your resume to the job you are applying for and leave out hobbies or personal details that do not directly relate to the job. More information about applying for specific types of jobs is included in chapter 7 of this guide.

Curriculum Vitae

A CV is a much more detailed overview of your experience and background, and may be up to 10 pages long. As a general rule, if you are not specifically asked for a CV, don't send one. You want the decision-maker to be able to focus on the material that will help you get the job.

If you do need a CV, here are the basic things you should include:

- Your contact information (name, address, telephone, fax, e-mail, etc.)

- Any professional certifications you have

- Education: Any degrees you have and the school you got each degree from

- Your academic and professional interests, especially the ones that would be most useful in the job you're applying for

- Past employment: Any work experience you have that relates to the job

- Any professional organizations you belong to and any offices you hold in them

- Awards, scholarships, prizes, etc.

- Articles you have published

- Service such as volunteer work, committees, etc.

- References: People who will speak highly of you

Biography

A biography is a write-up which explains why you are an expert on a particular topic. It may be only a few paragraphs or a single page.

Your biography should make you sound like a star. You can see plenty of examples of what a biography looks like by visiting speakers' websites. For example, if you go to **www.speaking.com** and look up speakers by topic, you will be given a list of names and short biographies of speakers who specialize in that topic. You can then click on a speaker's name to read a more detailed biography. The more detailed biography is what you would prepare for your information package. You can also see speaker Andrea Kulberg's biography in section 7.6 of this book for another example.

Check out the biographies of a variety of speakers so you can see the different ways your own biography could be done. Like a resume, your biography can be tailored for the specific position you are applying for.

Color Photograph

The photograph you use to sell yourself to prospective employers should be a professional portrait. A recommended size is 4" x 6", labelled on the back with your name and contact information (address, phone number, fax, e-mail, website).

It can be a head shot or one in which you are holding a prop related to what you speak about. For example, if you speak about time management, an effective prop would be an oversized clock.

Why Bother With a Photograph?

Speakers sometimes wonder why they have to include a photograph with their materials. "Aren't they judging me on my speaking ability?"

Certainly. But your appearance is also important to many prospective employers. (Some prospective employers such as universities will consider it irrelevant.) Most meeting planners want the person who will be delivering the keynote address at their conference to appear successful. Likewise, seminar companies expect the person who will be presenting their business programs to appear polished and professional.

Remember, one of the factors audiences use to judge a speaker's credibility is the speaker's appearance. A speaker who looks unprofessional reflects poorly on the person who hired the speaker. Your photograph reassures the person who is considering hiring you that you are a professional. Furthermore, your photograph can be used by the person who hires you to help promote your talk.

Your photograph may end up being used in an employee newsletter, on a conference brochure, in a newspaper ad, or a variety of other promotional material. Because people are more likely to read articles with photographs, the information promoting your talk will be more widely read, possibly resulting in higher attendance. Your photograph definitely serves a practical purpose!

Getting Photos

In addition to a head shot, it's a good idea to get some action shots of you speaking to include in your promotional materials. Your photographs should be shot in a studio and at a live presentation by a professional photographer. This is generally not the place to try to save a few dollars by having a relative with a camera take your picture (unless your relative happens to be a professional photographer). To find a photographer, you can check the Yellow Pages or ask for recommendations from friends. View samples of several photographers' work and ask for price quotes, including the cost per print.

One way to keep your costs down is to find a photographer who will sell you the negatives so you can make prints yourself. You may pay the photographer a higher fee up front, but over the long run you will probably save a great deal by having the prints made at a one-hour photo outlet. I have found the quality from the photo outlet I use to be very close to the quality from my photographer. The most significant difference is that the cost per print is five times lower from my photo outlet. As with any service you purchase, expect to shop around to find a photo outlet you'll be happy with.

One-Sheets

A one-sheet is a "brochure" printed on one or both sides of an 8 1/2" x 11" sheet of paper which promotes you and one of your programs. You can produce a separate one-sheet for each program that you present. A typical one-sheet may include one or more photos of you, a brief biography, topic description, benefits of the program, a partial list of clients, testimonials, and contact information.

In addition to including them in an information package, one-sheets are great for faxing to prospective employers. Speakers bureaus also like to use one-sheets to fax to their clients. If you are working with a bureau, leave the contact information off your one-sheet so they can fill in their own information, or print off copies with the bureau's information on them.

There are a variety of different styles of one-sheets used by successful speakers, ranging from desktop published in black and white to professionally designed in full color. On the facing page is a sample one-sheet I used to speak on management communications topics.

Sample One-Sheet

TAG GOULET
MANAGEMENT COMMUNICATIONS TRAINING

Imagine a workplace filled with peak performers–people who enjoy their work, communicate effectively, achieve outstanding results and go the extra mile for their employer. This is the kind of workplace Tag can help you create. She can teach your managers and supervisors how to increase your organization's productivity by:

- motivating employees
- improving morale
- delegating and empowering effectively
- successfully leading teams
- resolving conflicts
- coaching employees
- keeping top performers

Praise for Tag's presentations...

"Tag receives outstanding comments from our employees. They find the content extremely useful and are immediately able to use many new ideas both professionally and personally."
S. Hutton, ENMAX Corporation

"Valuable, humorous and very motivating. 'Chock full' of hints and wisdom that will save me time, effort and frustration."
L. Purdy, Department of National Defence

"I have attended many seminars and yours was the best value for the dollar that I have ever received. Not only was it chock full of useful and vital information—but it was entertaining as well."
J. Hutchins, Nanaimo Chamber of Commerce

"I've gained more practical, applicable knowledge through your programs than through any other educational experience."
Lori Benjamin, *Calgary Sun* columnist

Topics Include

- Skills for New Supervisors
- Keeping Valuable Employees
- Interpersonal Communication
- Programs customized for your group

Tag Goulet has trained and spoken in public to thousands of people in 24 cities. Her more than 15 years of management experience includes serving as vice-president of production for a company distributing products in 65 countries. A columnist for the Calgary Herald, her advice has also appeared in the United States Chamber of Commerce Magazine. Tag is a highly rated instructor of Management Communications at the University of Calgary and a contributor to several books.

Partial List of Clients

- American Management Association
- Fairmont Hotels & Resorts
- ENMAX Corporation
- City of Calgary
- Government of Canada

You can add your contact information or leave a blank space to allow speakers bureaus to add their contact information

According to Sheryl Roush, an internationally top-rated speaker, a well-designed one-sheet professional profile includes:

- Banner benefit statement at the top of layout

- Speaker's name (in a stylized type style)

- Full-body or 2/3 view action photo on one side

- Portrait photo on the other side (without a microphone)

- Defining statement of your unique or valuable expertise

- Program descriptions, titles (one paragraph, plus three to five bullet-pointed benefits)

- Results to be generated, bullet pointed under title

- Biography, credentials, publications and experiences

- Testimonials – rave reviews – with their names and organizations

- Signature look and feel, demonstrating your personality (perhaps a moniker)

- Logos for full NSA members (NSA, CAPS, ICF MPI, ASTD, etc.)

- Contact information (toll-free phone number, website, e-mail)

- And, if you're going to quote someone famous, quote yourself

- Optional: Your organization's logo placed at the bottom of the layout

Sheryl advises: "After your print design is ready, post it as a PDF file on your Web site, making it easy for quick download by meeting professionals who need to make that decision right now! This also enables you to make instant changes, and have bureau-friendly (without your contact information) versions. I post my general one-sheets (keynotes and workshops) and the topic-specific sheets on my homepage for immediate access and download."

You can see Sheryl's own fabulous one-sheets and read more about her at **www.SparklePresentations.com**. Sheryl has also created a 2 volume CD-ROM set called *Solid Gold Speaker One-Sheets*. It includes 66 PDF files plus video and sells for $59.95 at **www.sparklepresentations.com/store_sg_sos_cdr.asp**.

To see other speakers' one-sheets, check speakers' web pages or do a web search for "motivational speaker one-sheet PDF."

How to Get Fantastic Testimonial Letters

A "testimonial letter" is a reference letter from someone who has hired you to speak. A good testimonial letter can help you land other speaking engagements. A mediocre testimonial letter can actually hurt your chances of getting hired. No one wants to hire a mediocre speaker!

If you leave it up to the person who hired you to write a testimonial letter, they may miss some of the key points that can help you get hired by another employer.

Which reminds me of a story...

When my husband Clayton and I began teaching workshops for singles seeking a partner, one of the first presentations we did was a free talk to a local singles association on the topic "What does the opposite sex want?" It was part of a weekly "drop-in" series the association had been running for several years.

To promote our presentation we prepared an intriguing write-up for the association's newsletter and contacted the local newspaper to run a story before the event.

The night of our talk about 30 chairs were set out, the usual number required for the weekly presentations. Those chairs were filled long before the event was to begin, and people continued to stream in. By the time we started, almost 200 people had packed the room to hear our presentation. The standing-room-only crowd was the largest turnout in the association's history.

That night, the association made more money than they had ever before made at one of their presentations.

Most of the attendees were non-members who had read about our talk in the newspaper and paid to attend. After hearing our talk, many of the people who were attending for the first time decided to join the association and pay the annual membership fee.

The benefits continued long afterwards. So many new members joined as a result of our talk that the association raised the advertising rates in their newsletter. (As I discovered the next time I went to place an ad for our singles workshop!)

I wanted other potential employers to know about these results. I asked the event organizer to write a testimonial letter. She was a single mom who was also busy with work and volunteering, but she promised to do it as soon as she had time. Five weeks later the letter arrived. Here is much of what it said:

> *"We are continuing to enjoy successful Thursday evening Drop-Ins! Our committee has been pleased to see the attendance and positive feedback continue to grow.*
>
> *At this time I would like to acknowledge the important contribution you have made to this success. We feel that your willingness to offer your time and experience has been a major factor.*
>
> *Although we have not been able to express our appreciation in a financial way, we would again like to express our gratitude to you."*

It was a form letter.

What I learned from that experience is that many event organizers are too busy with their own lives to worry about writing the ideal letter for a speaker.

TIP: You are much more likely to get the type of testimonial you want – an extraordinary letter that can convince potential employers to hire you – if you write it yourself.

Simply suggest to the event organizer that you draft a letter for their approval. Most event organizers will be grateful for the offer. They want to help, but they would prefer that it not take too much effort. Drafting the letter yourself is a perfect win-win solution.

The letter you draft should emphasize all the value you brought to the organization you spoke for. Emphasize those things that potential employers are likely to see as benefits. And do NOT say anything about having spoken for free. You don't want potential employers thinking that's how much your speaking is worth. Furthermore, a good speech is a good speech, regardless of how much you were paid to give it.

If I were writing the testimonial letter myself it would have included comments such as the following:

I am writing to thank you for the outstanding presentation you gave to our group on September 20.

As a result of the promotion you did before the event, we had the largest turnout for a speaker in the ten-year history of our organization.

The standing-room-only crowd gave you fantastic ratings, and we sold 100 new memberships after your speech. Many of the people who joined told us it was because of how impressed they were with your talk. Among the comments we heard from participants were...

Optional Items

In addition to the items listed above, your information package can include anything else that will help you land the job. These items should help to establish you as an expert and communicate the benefits you would bring to an employer.

When deciding what else to include in your package, ask yourself: "Will this help convince someone to hire me?" If the answer is "yes," of course you should include it. If the answer is "maybe," include it only if your package contains very little.

If your package already contains a lot of material it's best to leave out the "maybes," because you don't want the strongest selling features to be buried under papers that aren't as important.

Items you can add to your package include:

Client List

Add your client list if it includes clients that are household names, or clients in the same industry as the prospective employer.

Newspaper and Magazine Clippings

These should ideally be about you, or written by you, and should relate to your speaking or expertise. If you haven't yet published anything, an alternative is to write an article and desktop publish it to make it appear like a newspaper or magazine article. Of course you can't claim to have published it, but someone taking a quick look through your folder might respond to the familiar format and read it.

Brochures

You can include brochures about you or relevant programs you offer. (For example, you would not send a management seminar company a copy of the brochure for an aromatherapy course that you teach.)

Promotional Gift

A promotional gift is any small item that can help a prospect remember you. This could be a pen, a postcard, or even a treat like chocolates. The more creative your gift, the more it will help you be noticed and remembered. If you decide to include a gift, it could be personalized with your name and contact information or it could simply be something that relates to what you speak about.

For example, when I was promoting relationship workshops, I included a pencil decorated with a color cartoon titled "Written on My Heart." Because it was unique and colorful, people hung onto it.

You may be able to find inexpensive gift items in local stationery stores. If you are looking for personalized items, you can do an Internet search for "promotional gifts" or check the Yellow Pages under "advertising."

Get Them to Open Your Package

If you want potential employers to look at your package, the key is to send your materials to people who are expecting them. One way to get permission is by making a phone call similar to one you would use to arrange a meeting, but ask for permission to send your package instead.

Knowing who to send it to is critical. Any package addressed to a department or "Dear Sir or Madam" can end up, like the packages in the bureau owner's basement, in an "open when there's time" pile.

The problem is that many of the people who could hire you simply do not have the time or the desire to browse through a pile of unsolicited packages on the slim chance they'll find the next speaking star. Many decision-makers know from past experience that the vast majority of the packages in that pile will be from amateurs. The odds of finding an excellent applicant among the "Dear Sir or Madam" pile are slim indeed.

A package that comes personally addressed to someone is treated completely differently. Addressed packages get opened—even if they are addressed to someone who no longer works in the office.

What if You Don't Have the Decision-Maker's Name?

What if you have contacted a prospective employer and find yourself "stuck" speaking to an assistant who won't give you the name of the decision-maker? The answer is to send your package and letter personally addressed to that assistant.

This person has the power to pass your package on to the decision-maker. If you make a good impression, she can go even further and actively promote you to her boss. ("Hey boss, this one looks good.") In many cases, the decision-maker will be more likely to pay attention. A decision-maker with a high level of trust in their assistant may even decide to hire you based on the assistant's recommendation.

An assistant will typically respond more positively to a package addressed to her than to "Head of XYZ Department." (By the way, she is much more likely than her boss to be the person who actually ends up opening the "Dear Sir or Madam" packages anyway.)

6.3.3   Other Ways to Approach Them

Direct Mail

The U.S. Postal Service has great information on direct mail including a guide to the ins and outs of sending business mail at **www.usps.com/ businessmail101**. There is also a comprehensive guide called "Direct Mail by the Numbers" which tells you how to harness the power of direct mail.

You can order it online at **www.usps.com/directmail/publications.htm**, or you can order it at your local post office.

Postcards

Some speakers follow up their packages with a postcard. Postcards are a quick and easy way to contact an employer, and they get read.

I know of one speaker who sends a postcard asking, "Have you received my package?" Chances are the employer has not received the package, because the speaker has not sent one! He says this technique saves him money because he is not sending a complete information package to people who are not interested. Furthermore, he claims to have a better response than from sending out complete packages.

You can get postcards made up at a local printer or use a supplier such as Modern Postcard at **www.modernpostcard.com**. Modern Postcard can produce 500 full-color promotional postcards for as little as $129. Their website offers some great tips on additional ways you can use postcards to market yourself.

Faxes

Another option is to fax out a letter to prospective employers who have given you permission to contact them (sending unsolicited faxes can get you in trouble). In this letter you would emphasize the benefits of hiring you, meeting with you, attending one of your presentations, or whatever your goal is.

A key to getting a response is to make it easy for the person you send your fax to. A great way to do that is to put check boxes at the bottom of the page so the prospective employer can simply check off what they would like to do and fax it back it you. You might have spaces for them to check off such items as:

❑ Please send me an information package.

❑ Please call to set up a meeting.

❑ Not interested at this time.

❑ I'm busy right now. Please contact me again in _____.

❑ I'm not the right person to contact. Contact _____.

In case the prospective employer is interested, make sure you leave a space for them to fill in their correct name, address (if they want a package), phone number, and e-mail so you can follow up.

6.3.4   Invite Them to See You Speak

The following story shows an incredibly effective way of marketing yourself:

Years ago, a reporter told me about a speaker named Barbara Coloroso who had written a book titled *Kids Are Worth It!* and had spoken before hundreds of thousands of people the previous year.

A week later I saw a newspaper ad: Barbara Coloroso (shown in photo) was coming to town to autograph copies of her book. I decided this was my chance to find out the secrets to her success as a speaker.

I sent her a fax telling her how much I admired her marketing savvy and her success as a speaker, and that I wanted to hire her for a consultation while she was in town – no matter what the cost. To my disappointment, she didn't respond. The day of the book signing arrived, and I decided to go to the bookstore anyway and introduce myself.

"So you're the one!" she said. She explained why she hadn't responded to my fax: "I really can't tell you about my marketing because my husband does it for me," she said. "But if you're willing to pay for the phone call, he would be happy to let you pick his brain."

That call was worth many times what it cost me. Her husband described how Barbara had gone from being a stay-at-home Mom to a speaker reaching hundreds of thousands of people a year. The most significant thing he told me was that when Barbara was just starting out, they organized unpaid speaking opportunities and invited decision-makers to see her speak. Barbara is a fantastic speaker, so when the people actually saw her, they wanted to hire her immediately. Those presentations launched her career. You can find out more about Barbara Coloroso at **www.kidsareworthit.com**.

What Barbara did is something you can do, too. An effective way to give prospective employers a taste of your abilities is to invite them to attend a small part of a full-day seminar.

Many decision-makers can't afford to give up a full day or even a half day to hear a new speaker, but they may be willing to spend an hour. Of course, when you contact them you have to convince them of the value of spending that hour with you.

EXAMPLE:

One speaker, who normally earns $7,000 per day, puts on seminars and invites decision-makers to attend for an hour free of charge. To ensure the room is packed with participants, he charges a low registration fee (under $150) and has friends sit in on the seminar. He starts his seminar at 8:30 a.m. and the prospective employers are invited to arrive at 9:00 a.m. When they arrive they are led quietly to seats at the back of the room.

For the next hour the speaker delivers his very best material. At 10:00 a.m., when he reaches the climax of his presentation—a point where the audience is eager for more—he stops for a coffee break. During the break he meets and mingles with the decision-makers.

Then his assistant breaks in to say that some of the seminar participants want to see him. (A good speaker will usually be in demand on the breaks.) He reluctantly says good-bye to the decision-makers and leaves his assistant to speak with them.

His assistant tells each of the decision-makers that the speaker is available for a limited number of speaking engagements and that she will be calling to follow up with them.

This technique has generated a tremendous amount of work for the speaker at his full fee. By having decision-makers attend part of his presentation, they can see for themselves how well he speaks. The usual fears a decision-maker may have about speakers (What if the speaker insults my audience? What if the speaker is boring?) are dispelled by seeing the speaker in action.

It isn't even necessary to hold your own seminars to use this technique. Any time you have a paid or unpaid speaking engagement, you can ask the event organizer for permission to invite a few "guests" to see your talk. In many cases, the event organizer will be happy to accommodate you and your guests.

6.3.5   Following Up

It is important to follow up after a decision-maker has seen you speak or received information from you. The reason is because no matter how good they think you are, they probably have many other tasks competing for their time and attention. Following up can help make working with you a higher priority for them.

You have heard the saying, "The squeaky wheel gets the oil." You could also say, "The appropriately persistent speaker gets the job." Being appropriate doesn't mean calling several times a day. It means calling a day or so after the decision-maker has heard you talk or received your package to explore what benefits you could bring them by working with their organization.

If they are too busy to talk when you call, ask when it would be a good time to call back, then make sure you do so. See the advice above about "Calling Potential Employers" for some tips you can use for your follow up calls, too.

What If a Decision-Maker Can't Attend?

No matter when your events are scheduled for, there will be some decision-makers who will not be able to attend. Some simply cannot find the time to spend an hour (plus travel time) listening to every speaker who is interested in working with them. Furthermore, you probably will not have many opportunities to travel around speaking or presenting seminars in all the cities where prospective employers are located.

So, how can you show these people how talented you are? How can you convince them that you are not one of the speakers they fear? The answer is to send them a demo.

6.4 Producing Demo Materials

To an employer, the next best thing to seeing you live is seeing you or hearing you on tape, so demo materials are effective promotional tools.

6.4.1 Producing a Video Demo

While it can be helpful for an employer to hear you on an audio tape or audio CD, most of them also want to see you. In fact, many employers won't even consider an application that doesn't include a video demo.

> **TIP:** To ensure your video can be viewed by as many people as possible, you should make it available on CD-ROM or DVD.

In most cases you will need a video demo (also known as a *demo video*) if you want to work with national seminar companies, get hired to speak at conferences, speak on cruise ships, or work with speakers' bureaus. The decision-makers in these organizations base their choices of speakers to a large extent on speaker videos.

You don't necessarily need a video if you are planning to work with corporations, teach continuing education courses, or work with local (as opposed to national) seminar companies. However, giving these prospective employers a video can help put you miles ahead of the competition. It communicates that you are an experienced professional and can show them how talented you are as a speaker.

EXAMPLE:
A video helped me when I applied to present media relations seminars through a small public relations firm. The person doing the hiring had never before received an audition video from someone interested in teaching one of their seminars. The day after she received my video she called to offer me the position, telling me how much she had enjoyed it and that my presentation style was exactly what they were looking for.

What Employers Expect in Your Video

Like the rest of us, people who hire speakers have been raised in an era of increasing sensory stimulation. From music videos to television shows, from theatrical movies to DVDs, the media we pay attention to are generally fast-paced, visually exciting, and come with a soundtrack.

The people who hire speakers have the same expectations for video demos. They want a broadcast-quality video that is exciting, dynamic, and powerful. Every day they may see speaker videos offering a variety of well-edited shots, attractive graphics, and professional music.

Producing a video with these qualities usually costs upwards of two thousand dollars. So what can you do if you are a beginner without several thousand dollars to spare?

Do-it-Yourself Video Demos

When you are just starting out, it is okay if your demo is simply a recording of all or part of a live presentation. The fact that it is not "broadcast-quality" is usually not significant. Thanks to the popularity of YouTube.com and the use of viewers' videos on CNN, it's no longer essential to have broadcast quality videos in order to make a positive impression.

However, it's usually best to avoid what some speakers have done with the speaker trying to pretend they are doing a live presentation, but actually delivering their talk to an empty room. Prospective employers like to hear laughter, applause, and other signs of audience approval.

Furthermore, employers know that someone who is able to comfortably deliver a presentation in front of a camera may become nervous and speak poorly in front of a group. So, if possible, make sure the presentation on your demo is actually performed in front of an audience.

> **TIP:** It's a good idea to record as many of your talks as you can. You will almost certainly improve over time as a speaker, so it's a good idea to have your best recent video to show prospective employers.

Here are some tips for recording your speech:

Get a Camera

Recording your presentation can be as simple as borrowing or renting a video camera and setting it up at the back of the room.

If you don't know someone with a video camera check the Yellow Pages under "video." Another option is to get the organization that is sponsoring your speech to arrange for the recording. Some tips on how to do this are included below under "Videos for Advanced Speakers."

Set up the Camera

To ensure the video is not jerky, put it on a tripod rather than having someone hold it. Before your presentation, practice delivering part of your speech while having someone watch you through the camera's viewfinder. The person watching you through the viewfinder should try to get as close a view of you as possible, while ensuring that you don't move out of camera range if you are walking around the stage during your talk.

Get Permission to Record

The presence of a camera can make some audience members nervous even if the camera is focused only on you, so before bringing in a video camera get the event organizer's approval. If you are doing a free talk, you might explain that you would like to record your speech to send to prospective employers. Assure the event organizer that the camera will be focused only on you, and when you start your presentation you can also let the audience know the camera is only on you.

If any members of the audience will be recorded, you will need to get written permission from them. You could designate one side of the room for those who do not want to be recorded, and the other side of the room for those who are willing to be recorded. For those who are willing, ask them to complete a simple form such as the one on the facing page.

Reviewing the Video

After your presentation, view the entire recording to find the best part to include on your demo. Your demo does not have to consist of your entire presentation from start to finish. In fact, many decision-makers will not watch more than 15 minutes of it. In most cases a 15- to 20-minute video is all you need.

If your speech opening was fantastic, your demo should start at the beginning of your talk. However, if your presentation was significantly

---

Sample Permission Form

I hereby give (insert your name) permission to use my photograph or videotape taken of me on (insert date) at (insert location) for promotional, online or commercial purposes. I am of legal age.

Name: _____

Signature: _____

Witness: _____

---

stronger in a later part of your talk, it may be better to start your demo there. Many prospective employers will start making judgments about your speaking ability within the first minute of viewing your video, so make sure you immediately grab their attention.

Make Copies of the Video

Once you know which part of the video you want to include in your demo, you can have it duplicated. If you have a CD burner on your computer you can make your own copies as you need them. (You can buy blank CDs at any office supply store.) Or, for a few dollars each you may be able to get it professionally duplicated along with a label, generic sleeve, and shrinkwrapping (plastic wrapping). Companies that offer video and CD duplication services can be found in the Yellow Pages.

> **TIP:** Don't get too many copies of your first demo duplicated because one of your future presentations may be much better. Depending on how many videos you plan to mail out to decision-makers, duplicating as few as 50 copies of your first demo may be most cost-effective.

A Low-Cost Option

You can get a broadcast-quality video relatively inexpensively by sharing costs with other speakers. Many video companies offer their services by the day or half-day, so several speakers can be recorded for the same cost as recording only one speaker.

If you are speaking at an event with a number of other speakers, such as a convention, you could see if some of those speakers would like to split the cost of recording.

If you don't have any such speaking engagements scheduled, you can "create" an event of your own and arrange a half-day or full-day program with a number of different speakers presenting sessions of perhaps 20 minutes each. Organizing this event would involve a number of tasks including: finding the other speakers, booking a location, arranging for recording, and getting an audience.

To ensure a positive response from the audience, it is a good idea for each participating speaker to invite people they know who would be willing to respond enthusiastically to each speaker and remain for the entire event. (You don't want audience members leaving as soon as they have seen their friend speak.)

Participating speakers would split the cost of the recording and other expenses such as the location rental. Each would then make separate arrangements with the video company for duplication.

Videos for Advanced Speakers

When you are ready to take your career to the level of a full-time professional speaker, you are ready for a complete video demo. A professional video demo has the following qualities:

- broadcast quality (HD or high definition will soon be the norm)

- professional graphics

- music

- voice-over by a professional announcer

- powerful opening

- variety of camera shots

- combination of live action (you presenting) and studio shots (you speaking to the camera)

Live Action Segments

For your live action segments, you can include clips from a variety of different talks. However, your clips need to be long enough to give the prospective employer a good feel for your content. Ideally, these live action segments should represent your best material and include some short powerful stories.

These segments should also include shots of the audience listening intently and being moved by your presentation. In other words, your video will have a greater impact if you can show your audience reacting to your talk with laughter, tears, gasps, cheers, enthusiastic applause, or any other powerful, positive response.

Some speakers like to show audiences of a variety of sizes, while others prefer to show only large audiences. What you include on your video will depend on the image you want to present. Do you want to show your adaptability to groups of different sizes? Then show a variety of audiences. Do you want to emphasize that you are a successful professional? Then you may want to show only large audiences.

Some speaker videos also include a complete presentation at the end, so the decision-maker can see that you do a great job throughout your entire speech. There are several ways to get video footage of your presentations.

- A client may ask you if it is okay to record your speech. If this happens, you can give them permission on the condition that they make a master (or a copy produced directly from the master footage) available to you for your video demo. This can also be an opportunity to add to your fee. You could allow recording rights in return for an additional fee such as $1 per employee or as much as 50 percent of your fee.

- If the client is not planning to record your speech, you can suggest it to them. For example, you could explain that the video might be useful for absentees, training, or promotional purposes. In this case you could negotiate a fee or offer to waive your regular recording rights fee in exchange for a submaster.

- Another option, of course, is to hire someone to record the event for you. You might want to do this if you are speaking to a particularly large group or otherwise feel that footage of this event would be useful for your demo.

TIP: Whenever you shoot live footage, remember to get releases from audience members giving permission for you to film them.

Other Content

You can vary the live action shots with studio segments of you speaking about yourself and your program. The studio segments are your opportunity to speak as if you were speaking directly to the decision-maker. These segments should emphasize the benefits of hiring you.

For your staged studio segments, you can find a local company to record you, or try a company such as Chesney Communications (**www.videocc. com**) that has worked with a variety of speakers.

Some speakers also include testimonials of people saying good things about the speaker. Even if you have never seen another speaker video, you have probably seen testimonials in TV infomercials. However, for a speaker video, testimonials should be included only if they are from well-known organizations or individuals.

To be perceived as a professional, it is better to leave out testimonials altogether than to include ones from unknown people, who a decision-maker may assume are simply friends you found to say nice things about you.

Editing and Producing Your Demo

There are a variety of services available to help you produce a top-notch professional video demo.

To edit and produce your video, you may be able to use a company that has done some of your recording. You could also ask other speakers for recommendations or simply check the Yellow Pages under "video." If you want to save on editing costs you might be able to use the facilities of a local cable TV company to review your footage. But to put it all together, you will probably want to use the services of a pro.

To save on the cost of buying music, you can purchase "royalty-free" music, which means you are free to use the music without paying additional fees to the songwriter. Music Bakery, for example, offers CDs of varying types of music, from jazz to rock to classical. For as little as $59 you can buy a CD with a selection of music you can use in your video demos. You can listen to clips of music tracks at their website, **www.music bakery.com**. You can also call them at (800) 229-0313.

TIP: You can see some videos by doing a search for professional speaker or motivational speaker at **www.YouTube.com**. Notice what you find effective and how other speakers promote themselves, for example, by having their name and web address appear on the screen.

6.4.2   Producing Audio Tapes or CDs

An audio demo is optional, but worth considering. While it can't take the place of a video demo, it can help strengthen your promotional package. Although most prospective employers will want to see you before they hire you, your audio tape or CD can provide further evidence of your speaking skills.

TIP: If you speak on more than one topic, it is a good idea to produce separate audio demos for each topic.

The Content of an Audio Demo

Your audio demo should ideally be about 10 minutes long. It may include:

- Music

- A brief introduction from an announcer

- Eight minutes or so of one of your presentations

- Audience reaction (laughter, applause, etc.)

- Conclude with the announcer explaining how to contact you

Or you could start your audio demo with a powerful part of your presentation including audience reaction, then have the announcer come on. You could then continue with short clips from your presentation alternating with comments from the announcer. Like your video demo, your audio demo should represent your best material and include some short powerful stories. You could also include an entire speech at the end of the tape, introduced by the announcer.

Recording Your Speeches

Perhaps the easiest and most cost-effective way to record your speeches is with a cassette recorder that you slip into your pocket and carry as you speak. Electronics stores such as Radio Shack sell a variety of recorders. You should be able to find several different models for about $60-80, or even less if they're on sale. Another option which can provide superior sound is a minidisc recorder manufactured by companies such as Sony or Sharp. You can find disc recorders at electronics stores for a few hundred dollars.

To ensure the recorder picks up your voice, you will also need a lapel or lavaliere microphone (a microphone you pin on your jacket). These are available for about $30. You will also need tapes to record on. To avoid disruption to your talk, find tapes that can record until you take a break, perhaps 90 or 120 minutes in length.

If you have the budget, you might even consider buying your own portable recording studio. For example, Expert Magazine offers a product for $895 which you can read about at **www.expertmagazine.com**.

Getting Copies Made

As with your video demo, you do not want to produce thousands of audio demos because you may decide to update it. Instead, it may be most cost-effective to start with about 100 tapes or CDs. If you shop around you can find companies that can duplicate 100 audio tapes or CDs for about one dollar each. You can find companies that duplicate audio materials in the Yellow Pages, or do an online search for "duplication services." For example, CD/DVD Now at **www.cddvdnow.com** is one company that offers to duplicate small quantities of CDs or DVDs quickly and affordably.

Of course, you could make copies yourself for only the cost of the tapes if you copy them yourself on a dual cassette recorder, or for only the cost of the CDs if you have a CD burner on your computer. However, if you want to make the best impression, a professional duplication company can provide you with attractive packaging.

Contacting employers by mail and phone using the methods described above should help you land some great speaking opportunities. But it's even better if you can get prospective employers to approach you.

6.5 How to Get Employers to Approach You

If an employer approaches you and is seriously interested in working with you, getting the job can be easy.

> **EXAMPLE:**
> One day I received an e-mail from a woman who was chairing a conference. She briefly described the event and added: "We are looking for a keynote speaker who is available on both October 19 and 20. Could you let me know if you are available and what your fee structure is?"
>
> I phoned and reached her voice mail. While some speakers might have kept calling until they could speak with her in person, I happened to be too busy for telephone tag. I left a brief message saying I would be delighted to speak and told her my fee. A few days later she phoned back to say the conference committee had met and decided to hire me.

In this case I got a high-paying keynote speaking job without giving the employer an information package, a video, or even a one-sheet. I didn't have to "jump through hoops," attend meetings, or make follow-up phone calls. It was not the first time I have experienced this. I have been approached a number of times by employers who were seriously interested in working with me. In each case, my effort to get these jobs was minimal because the employers had already decided to hire me.

These employers heard about me through a number of different means. In the example above, the decision-maker had read a newspaper column I had published in the Saturday business section of a newspaper. There are many other ways to get approached for a speaking job. The most effective ways to get an employer to approach you include: getting media publicity, getting published, giving free speeches, and presenting your own seminars.

The reason these methods can be so effective is because they establish you as "an expert." As a result, the employer may decide you are the only choice or the preferred choice for the job. The information in this section will give you some ideas on how you can use these opportunities to promote yourself for future speaking engagements.

6.5.1   The Importance of Being "An Expert"

As was explained in section 2.1.4 of this guide, in many cases it is possible to become an expert on a topic within only two weeks.

However, being an expert is not enough to get you hired. What is just as important is to be *seen* as an expert. Here's why. Imagine you are speaking with a potential employer:

EMPLOYER: What do you speak about?

YOU: I speak about Interpersonal Communications.

EMPLOYER: Great! That's what we're looking for. What are your credentials to speak on this topic?

YOU: Well, I've been studying Interpersonal Communications for the past two weeks...

Would *you* hire someone with these credentials? Of course not! Now imagine instead that you could say any or all of the following in response to, "What are your credentials?"

- "I have spoken on this topic numerous times to groups like yours."

- "I'm the author of *How to Improve Your Interpersonal Communications.*"

- "I have a Master's (or Ph.D.) degree in this area."

- "As an interpersonal communications expert I have been interviewed by media outlets in New York, Los Angeles, Houston, Chicago..."

- "More than 100,000 people have heard my advice on this topic."

Wouldn't you rather hire someone with credentials like these? So what if your own credentials look nothing like these? Well that's one of the many areas where this guide can help you. Read on to discover how you can get similar credentials as quickly as possible.

A Faster, Easier Way to Get a Degree

Earning a Master's degree or Ph.D. in an area related to what you speak about can certainly help establish your expertise. However, earning degrees the conventional way can take many years.

There Are Alternatives

When I say "alternatives," I'm not talking about sending $100 to a company in return for a phony "degree" to hang on your wall. That can get you into big trouble. As you become more well known as a speaker, it's more likely that someone may look into your background, so your degrees had better be real.

A much better alternative is to earn a degree from a "non-traditional" college. A non-traditional college is one that allows you to study at your own pace or through "distance learning" from the comfort of your own home.

More than half of U.S. colleges offer distance learning through online programs or correspondence. For example, you could earn an MBA (Masters of Business Administration) degree from a reputable school like Duke University or Syracuse University through distance learning.

Your Life Experience May Be Worth College Credit

You may even be able to earn a significant part of a degree based on your "life experience." In other words, some colleges will grant you course credits for things you have already done.

The *Bears' Guide to Earning Degrees by Distance Learning*, by John B. Bear, Ph.D. and Mariah P. Bear, M.A., lists 100 things that could be worth credit for life experience learning, depending on such factors as the college and the degree program. Among the items listed are "writing a speech" and "making a speech."

For more information about non-traditional programs you can use a guide like Bear's or contact colleges directly.

6.5.2   Get Media Publicity

Radio and Television

Imagine being able to tell potential employers that you have been interviewed by media outlets across the country.

Getting interviews is easier than many people imagine. And the good news is that you don't have to travel to New York, Los Angeles, or Chicago to speak with the media in those cities. You could sit in your kitchen in your bathrobe and slippers and give interviews to radio stations over the telephone. And if you're booked on a major TV talk show, your travel expenses may be covered by the show.

The Low-Budget Way to Get Interviews

The low budget but time-consuming way to get interviews is to contact stations directly to let them know you are available for an interview. The people to contact are talk show producers, news directors, or morning show hosts, depending on who you think would be most interested in your topic.

When you contact them, be sure to emphasize how much the show's audience will benefit from an interview with you. Remember, shows want dynamic, interesting guests.

Also, keep in mind that many station employees are overworked and underpaid. If you can make their job easier you are much more likely to land an interview. The best way to make their job easier is to include a list of "frequently asked questions" with the letter or news release you send them. This is a list of questions that you think listeners might like the answers to. For example, to promote our workshop for singles I prepared a list of questions like "What are the best places to meet people?" The questions I prepared were usually the ones I was asked on the air.

There are a variety of ways to find contact information for radio and TV outlets. An excellent one for radio is Radio Locator's searchable online directory of over 10,000 radio stations at **www.radio-locator.com**. To find links to television station websites across the U.S. visit the Gebbie Press website at **www.gebbieinc.com/tvintro.htm**. Look for the "Contact Us" section to find contact information.

The Easier Way to Get Interviews

A faster, easier, but more expensive way to get interviews is by placing an ad in the *Radio-TV Interview Report: The Magazine Producers Read to Find Guests* (*RTIR*). Shortly after I advertised in *RTIR*, I had long-distance interviews with dozens of radio stations, and was able to tell potential employers I had done media interviews "from Alaska to Alabama."

RTIR, which consists of ads promoting people who are available to be interviewed, is distributed three times per month to more than 5,000 radio and TV talk show producers in the United States (there are a few Canadian shows on their list, too).

As a result of such interviews, offers of speaking engagements may follow. For example, James Malinchak (**www.malinchak.com**) says he could not get on radio or TV until advertising with *RTIR*. His first interview after advertising generated three paid speaking engagements.

Even if your media appearances don't directly result in speaking engagements, it can still enhance your credibility with potential employers. Add up the audiences of all the shows you appear on, and you may soon be able to say that more than 100,000 or half a million or even millions of people have heard your advice.

RTIR advertising rates start at around $550 for a half-page ad. Their experts will write the ad for you at no extra cost. To get a free media kit with a copy of *RTIR* and information about advertising, call 1-800-553-8002, ext. 408. As an advertiser, you can also get a listing on the *RTIR* website. Visit **www.rtir.com** and click on "Become a Guest."

Other websites that list guests who are available for talk shows include the following (all charge a fee to be listed):

- *Authors and Experts*
  www.authorsandexperts.com

- *Expert Magazine*
  www.expertmagazine.com

- *Experts.com*
  www.experts.com

- *Guestfinder*
  www.guestfinder.com

- *Yearbook of Experts*
  www.expertclick.com

Advertising your availability for interviews can be expensive, as you'll see from exploring the sites above, and it may not generate results for all speakers.

Which reminds me of a story...

Years ago I hired a company to deliver flyers door-to-door to advertise a seminar I had coming up. (I foolishly did not consider the environmental implications.) The company that distributed the flyers told me that a one percent response rate was about average.

With 10,000 flyers being distributed, I was confident I would receive about 100 registrations in return for my $1,000 investment. I didn't. The flyers generated a single $50 registration, a loss of almost all the money I had invested in the flyers. When I asked the company what had happened, they answered, "Well, companies like Wal-Mart get a two percent response and small companies like yours get a zero percent response, so it all averages out to about one percent."

The lesson: even if an advertising vehicle gets results for people and companies that are already household names, it may not necessarily get results for you, so consider any monetary investments carefully.

No matter where you advertise, if your topic isn't interesting to the media, you may not get results. In some cases you may want to advertise because you feel a listing can give you credibility by itself. For example, if you advertise with ExpertClick, you will also be included in the impressive sounding *Yearbook of Experts, Authorities and Spokespersons.*

However, if getting interviewed is your goal, you may want to check with others who have advertised to see if your type of topic is one that actually gets interviews. Send a polite e-mail (you'll find contact information at the site) which includes the question, "How many interviews have you had as a result of your ad at _____?"

During the Interview

Whenever you are booked for a radio or TV show, arrange beforehand to have the interviewer say that you are a speaker and mention your telephone number and web address. If you are going to be appearing on TV, ask if they will display your contact information on the screen at some point during your interview.

What you say during the interview can also help to promote you. For example:

INTERVIEWER: What do you think is the biggest concern in this area?

YOU: I find the audiences at my speaking engagements are usually most concerned with...

You may even be able to throw in a mention of your web address:

YOU: That's one of the things I cover at my website, www.me.com. What I say there is...

Of course, bear in mind that mentioning your website works best if you have a short, memorable domain name (see section 6.5.4 on websites below). It would sound ridiculous to say, "As I explain at my website, http://www.myinternetcompany.com/mypages/me.html..."

Newspaper and Magazine Publicity

A single story about you in a daily newspaper or popular magazine could result in thousands of dollars worth of speaking engagements. That's because it can give you instant credibility. After all, your expertise is being reported by an independent journalist. It's no wonder a free story can generate many times more business than a paid advertisement.

As I have discovered on many occasions, employers who call after seeing a newspaper or magazine story are typically ready to hire. A decision-maker may read the paper, see the story about you, and decide you are the expert who can provide their company with what they need. You then become the employer's "preferred" speaker for an upcoming event.

Consider Subscribing to PR Leads

PR Leads is a service that notifies you by email about reporters who need to interview experts for stories they are writing. Every day they get upwards of 100 requests from reporters for top daily newspapers, like the *New York Times* and *Washington Post,* as well as leading business publications like *The Wall Street Journal,* top women's magazines like *Redbook* and *Glamour,* and leading business-to-business publications.

You can subscribe to PR Leads for $99 per month and includes 30 days of email coaching. More information is available from Dan Janal at **www.prleads.com**.

Send Out a Press Release

One way to get a story written about you is to send a press release (also called a "news release") to a writer, magazine editor, or the editor of the appropriate section of the newspaper. Depending on what you speak on, that might be the Business section, the Lifestyle section, or another part of the paper. You can find names and addresses of editors in reference directories at the local library or through the publication's website. You can find newspaper websites at **www.newspaperlinks.com**.

Your press release should be written so that it could be published "as is." Read the magazine or section of the paper where you would like to be published and use a similar writing style for your own news release. Following are some tips for writing a press release. Additional advice can be found online at **www.publicityinsider.com/release.asp**.

- Make sure the press release is newsworthy. For example, you could write about an upcoming event you'll be speaking at.

- Give your press release a strong lead paragraph that answers the six main questions: who, what, where, when, why, and how.

- Include factual information about yourself and your services. Remember, a press release should read like a news story, not an advertisement.

- Keep it short. Aim for a maximum of 500 words.

- Include your contact information at the end of the press release so that reporters and readers can reach you.

Invite a Reporter to Hear You Speak

The most effective way I have found to get newspaper publicity is to invite a newspaper reporter to attend a speech or seminar. A good way to invite the media is by sending a "pitch letter."

A pitch letter is a letter suggesting a story idea and why you believe it would be of interest to the newspaper's readers. It can be sent by mail, fax, or e-mail. You can also send it together with a media kit (your information package).

For best results, send it to a specific writer or editor who you believe might be interested in doing a story about you. For example, if you see a story about a speech or seminar, you could write to the reporter who covered it. Let them know you enjoyed their story and say you are writing to propose they cover another event which might interest their readers. Then give them a few details about your event and why it would interest their readers.

Sample Pitch Letter

Dear (insert first name of editor):

"The Singles Workshop" is coming to Toronto.

On Saturday, September 17, we are presenting a workshop for singles seeking a partner at the Sheraton Centre of Toronto.

Because more than one-third of Toronto adults are single, the workshop's tips on how to find a partner may interest many of your readers. Some of those tips are included in the enclosed package. Some are unusual, but even your readers who disagree should find the information interesting.

Your readers might also be interested in a feature story about the workshop, written from the point of view of a (insert name of newspaper) writer who attended the workshop.

If you want more details, or if you would like to send a writer to the workshop as our guest, please phone us toll-free at (800) 555-5555.

6.5.3   Get Published

Being a published author gives a tremendous boost to your credibility. "Yeah, right," you may be thinking, "All I have to do is write a book and find someone to publish it!" Well, that's one way to get published, but it's certainly not the only way. In this section you will discover several faster, easier ways to become a published author.

Publishing the Conventional Way

Publishing a book can be a time-consuming process if you do it the conventional way. Once the manuscript is written, it can take six months or more to find a publisher, then another 18 months from the time the publisher accepts the manuscript until it's finally in print. Sure it can help your credibility, but it's not exactly quick.

However, if this is something you want to do, you can find a list of publishers and the kinds of books they are looking for in *The Writers' Market*, a print and online publication available from Writers' Digest books. Check your library, bookstore, or **www.writersmarket.com**.

Self-Publish a Book

A much faster way to get a book published is to self-publish. Self-publishing is simply contracting with a printing company to produce your book. You can find printers that specialize in helping self-publishers by typing "self-publishing" into your favorite search engine.

There are many successful speakers and authors who have self-published. For example, John Gray, author of *Men Are From Mars, Women Are From Venus,* self-published his early books. Gray's *What You Feel, You Can Heal* was originally published in 1984 through his Heart Publishing Company.

Self-publishing can be expensive. It can cost thousands of dollars to print even 500 copies of a book. Depending on length, you might spend about $2.00 or so per book, assuming you print 1,000-2,000 copies (a recommended starting point for speakers who self-publish). However, you may be able to earn back much more by selling your book at your speeches. (More information about selling books and other products at your speeches is covered in section 9.2 of this guide.)

Can self-publishing a book add to your credibility? It certainly can – provided you do not volunteer the fact that your book is self-published. (Of course you would say it was self-published if you are asked.)

The reality is that many people perceive self-published books to be less impressive than "real" published books. No matter how outstanding your book was, a potential employer may believe it was "not good enough" to be accepted by a publishing house.

A good idea is to create a name for your publishing business. An appropriate publishing company name for the book above might be something like "Communication Publications." Make sure you create an original name and not one already in use by someone else.

See section 5.1.1 of this book for help with choosing a business name.

Publishing on Demand and Subsidy Publishing

A recent development is publishing books "on demand." In this form of publishing the author pays a company that prints copies of the book as orders come in. (The author's contribution is called a "subsidy.")

Unlike self-publishing, where the author keeps all the profits, publishing on demand typically pays the author a royalty (a percentage of the revenue from books sold). If you want to explore this option, you can find companies that offer this service by typing "subsidy publishing" or "publishing on demand" into a search engine. One popular print on demand company is Lulu at **www.lulu.com**.

Before paying any company to publish your book, thoroughly review their contract and ask for references. Also find out what they will do to market your book. Do they seem to earn most of their revenue from selling books or from authors' subsidies? Some authors have been disappointed by subsidy publishers that sold virtually no copies of their book.

Self-Publish a Booklet or Special Report

If you haven't written enough to publish a complete book, or if self-publishing a book is simply too expensive, a faster, cheaper alternative is to publish a booklet or special report.

Your booklet could be as simple as a few sheets of paper printed on both sides, folded in half and stapled in the middle. You can print booklets in any quantity quickly and inexpensively at a local printer such as Kinko's or Staples. For example, you might be able to have 50 copies of a short booklet published for less than $25. Another option is to create a special report, which could be the same information contained in your booklet, in PDF format.

There's no reason why *How to Improve Your Interpersonal Communications* couldn't be the title of a booklet or special report. You could then legitimately say that you are the author of *How to Improve Your Interpersonal Communications,* published by Communication Publications.

> **TIP:** Although this is a great technique for getting your foot in the door, it is not a way to "fool" people into thinking you are an expert if you really are not. Some potential employers will ask for a copy of your publication. So make sure you write a booklet packed with useful information and expert advice.

Publish a Newsletter

A great way to become a published author, and get a marketing tool in the process, is to publish a newsletter. You could then add to the list of your credentials something like "Editor, *Interpersonal Communication Quarterly* (or whatever you call your newsletter)."

Your newsletter can be long or short (even a single sheet of paper printed on both sides), photocopied or printed with color and graphics. You could publish it monthly, quarterly, annually, or however frequently you wish.

The content could consist of your own articles or you could fill it entirely with articles written by other people (used with their permission, of course). One way to get free articles from experts is to contact published authors. Many authors are happy to submit articles to newsletters in return for a paragraph promoting their book at the end of the article.

The fastest way to contact a published author is to send a letter addressed to them c/o the Editorial Department of their publishing house. You can find the publisher's address at the front of most books or check out **www.lights.com/publisher**, which has a list of publishers from all over the world.

To find out more about printing your own newsletter, contact your local printer or copy center like Kinko's, Office Depot, or Staples.

In addition to publishing a print version of your newsletter, you could publish an online version. Some tips for developing your own website are included further on in this section.

Write Articles or Columns

One of the best ways to establish yourself as an expert and promote yourself to prospective employers is to write articles or columns for newspapers, magazines, or newsletters.

You could write articles on any topic related to your niche, or propose an "Ask the Expert" column where you would answer questions from readers. If you write a column, the length and frequency will depend on the publication. You might write a weekly 500-word column for a local newspaper, or a monthly 1,000-word column for a newsletter or magazine.

While it can be tough to break into large daily newspapers, there may be an opportunity to write for smaller newspapers or magazines. There are literally thousands of magazines on a wide range of topics such as business, health, parenting, travel, and more. Many magazines accept submissions from freelance writers.

Unless you are already an established freelance writer, it's usually a waste of your time to try to sell articles to popular magazines such as *Reader's Digest, Time, Fortune,* or *Cosmopolitan.* Magazines like these are flooded with thousands of submissions every month, so the odds of having your article accepted for publication are almost non-existent.

You are more likely to have your article accepted if you submit it to smaller or lesser-known publications. Such publications may actually bring you more business as a speaker than the larger ones. For example, if you speak on sales strategies, you are more likely to reach potential employers if you write for magazines with titles such as *Sales and Marketing News* or *Professional Selling.*

You can find a listing of magazines and their guidelines for writers in *The Writers' Market,* a print and online publication. Check your library, bookstore, or **www.writersmarket.com**.

Many smaller publications are hungry for well-written articles that provide value to their readers. In many cases, the writer's background doesn't matter. For example, *The Canadian-American Law Journal* (which has since changed its name) usually published articles written by lawyers. However, when I sent them a well-researched article that they felt would interest their readers, they published it despite the fact that I do not have a law degree.

Make sure your articles or column provides valuable information to the publication's readers. As with press releases, articles that sound like an ad for your services are not likely to get published.

Whenever you write an article, include a short biographical paragraph at the end which says that you speak on the topic of the article and includes your telephone number, e-mail address, and website. Many editors are happy to publish a brief biographical paragraph, especially if you have written the article for free.

Produce Audio and Video Materials

Another way to become a published author is by writing your own audiovisual materials. As with books, you can find a conventional publisher to produce your videos or CDs, or you can self-publish.

If you are interested in finding a publisher, a good place to start looking is Publishers' Catalogs, the number one site for finding publishers on the web. At Publishers' Catalogs you can find information about publishers in a wide variety of categories, including "Audio," "Film/Video" and "Multimedia CD." Visit **www.lights.com/publisher/db/formats**.

You can also self-publish your own audio or video programs. More information about producing your own audiovisual materials is included in section 9.2.

6.5.4   Get a Website

Another way to "get published" is to produce your own Internet site. As many successful speakers have discovered, a website can help position you as an expert and enhance your credibility with potential employers.

If your budget is limited, you may be able to put up free webpages through your Internet Service Provider (the company that gives you access to the Internet). Contact them for details about how to put up your own website. It will probably have an address like: http://www.yourcompany.com/yourpages/index.html

It's preferable to get your own domain name such as http://www.your name.com because it makes you appear to be more serious about your speaking career. There are a number of sites where you can search for and register a domain name. One such site is **www.godaddy.com**, which also provides "hosting" services.

You can design your own web pages using a program like Front Page, or hire someone to design your site for you. Check your favorite search engine or your local Yellow Pages under "Internet." Remember to ask for references and get a price quote in writing.

What to Include on Your Website

The following items at your website can help establish your credibility:

- Your photograph: a headshot and some photos of you "in action" speaking before an audience are ideal. (Have photos taken at one of your free talks.)

- A summary of your programs and the benefits they offer to potential clients. (See section 2.5 of the guide for specific ideas.) You can also see the site I used to promote my communication programs at **www.FabJob.com/tag.html**.

- A "label" that sums up how you want potential employers to see you. To give some examples from star speakers: Anthony Robbins is "America's Results Coach," Mark Victor Hansen is "The Master Motivator," and Patricia Fripp is "A Speaker for All Reasons." You are what you call yourself.

- Testimonials from satisfied clients such as the ones you have done free talks for. (Don't volunteer the fact that you spoke for free!)

- Useful information, such as articles, stories, or quotations to add to your credibility and give potential employers a sense of your style.

- Audio or video "samples" of your speaking.

- A way to contact you, including at least your company name, telephone number and e-mail address. (This should be on every page.)

- To build up a contact list, you could offer a free e-mail newsletter, and include a place at your website where visitors can subscribe. You can send out e-newsletters inexpensively through a company such as Constant Contact at **www.constantcontact.com**. The cost starts at $15 per month for a list of up to 500 people, and a free trial is available.

For more ideas, check out the websites of successful speakers. You will find some successful speakers listed in section 2.4.

Other Online Promotion

If you work with a speakers bureau (see chapter 8), they will typically publish information about you at their website. However, they may have hundreds of speakers on their website, so your listing may not result in speaking engagements. Most reputable bureaus, such as Speakers Platform at **www.speaking.com**, list speakers free of charge. Other bureaus charge a "registration fee" of hundreds of dollars with no guarantee of work. That money would be better spent on your own website. If you are willing to pay to be listed at other sites, you can find some sites that list speakers and other experts in section 6.5.2.

6.5.5   Network With Decision-Makers

It's a fact: people are more likely to do business with people they know and like. If you establish friendly personal relationships with decision-makers, you will come to mind when they need someone to speak.

One of the best ways to network is by joining an association that decision-makers belong to. For example, if you want to speak at conferences you can join an association of meeting planners. Chapter 7 includes some specific suggestions of different types of groups you could join.

The most important thing to determine when you are looking at joining an association is whether the people who attend the group's events are actually decision-makers. In fact, many networking organizations attract far more "sellers" than "buyers." This means that the people you are networking with may only be interested in what they might be able to sell to you.

EXAMPLE:
Shortly after I joined the local Chamber of Commerce, I decided to attend a networking luncheon with my partner Clayton. We sat at different tables so we could meet as many people as possible. The people at my table included a life insurance salesperson, a real estate agent, a financial planner, and four other self-employed businesspeople who were hoping to find new clients. Clayton's table had exactly the same mix of occupations.

In fact, your local Chamber of Commerce can be an excellent networking vehicle, however, simply attending "networking" functions is not enough in many cases to make an impact on decision-makers.

To make the most out of your membership in an association, there are several things you can do to raise your profile, including:

- Serve on a committee

- Write articles for the association newsletter

- Offer to give presentations on topics of interest to the members

- Do volunteer work that will bring you into contact with other members

- Run for election to the Executive Committee

The more involved you are in the association, the more likely you are to connect with decision-makers. No matter what your level of involvement, you can still make the most of your membership by attending events and meeting people. Here are a few tips on how to effectively network:

- Before you network, set goals for yourself. Do you want to network with a certain number of people? Do you want to talk to people from certain industries?

- Plan to visit as many networking groups as possible, but avoid networking somewhere if you know ahead of time that you are unlikely to get anything out of it.

- At a networking event, don't be afraid to introduce yourself to other people. Be outgoing! Don't wait for them to come to you.

- Rather than trying to "sell" yourself, ask people about themselves. Aim to build mutually-rewarding relationships.

- Always have plenty of business cards on you. And don't hesitate to ask for someone else's card. You never know when you might want to look them up.

- Follow through on the contacts you make. Remind the person where you met them, say you enjoyed talking to them, and ask if you can get together again to share ideas.

6.5.6   Get Free Speaking Engagements

In many professions, there's the classic dilemma: You can't get a job without experience, but you can't get experience without a job. The speaking profession doesn't have that problem. You can get plenty of experience before you ever land your first paid speaking job.

The way to get experience is by speaking for free. Of course your goal is to earn money as a speaker, so you won't be doing this for long. However, even a few unpaid speaking engagements can give you what you need to start earning a living as a speaker.

Furthermore, many speakers find that much of their paid speaking work comes from doing other speeches. Even if there are no prospective employers in a particular audience, someone who hears you may recommend you to an employer.

Groups You Can Speak To

Many organizations are eager for guest speakers. To get free speaking engagements, ask everyone you know if they belong to any groups that ever use guest speakers. Whenever you get a "yes" answer, ask them who to contact to volunteer your services. (If they don't know, find out who the group's president is and contact him or her.)

Not sure who to ask for contacts? Start with your parents, brothers, sisters, aunts, uncles, in-laws, other relatives, friends, acquaintances, spouse's friends, relatives' friends, neighbors, customers, co-workers, former co-workers, people you meet at parties or networking events—in other words, ask EVERYONE. Many adults belong to at least one group that uses and needs guest speakers.

When you're speaking with people, ask if they belong to any:

- service clubs (e.g. Rotary Club or Kiwanis Club)

- business organizations (e.g. the Chamber of Commerce)

- professional associations (e.g. Executive Women International)

- ethnic and cultural organizations

- networking and breakfast clubs

- charitable organizations

- hobby and special interest clubs

If you were to check your local Yellow Pages under a category such as "Associations" you might find scores of groups listed. However, many groups do not have a Yellow Pages listing, and you will almost certainly have more success getting speaking engagements through word of mouth than by calling organizations listed in the phone book.

Many organizations are selective about who they let speak to their members. Most groups do not want speakers who will deliver a strong sales pitch or political message. So make sure when you speak with the event organizer (the person who can book you to speak) that you emphasize the benefits of your speech for the audience. (Benefits are covered in detail in section 2.5 of the guide.)

What You Get Out of It

As mentioned, you will not be speaking just for the practice (although it's great for that too). Instead, you will be speaking in return for important aids to your career. For example, after you speak to a group you can include it on your resume, you can ask for referrals from the event organizer, and you can get testimonials.

One type of testimonial is the "testimonial letter." This is a reference letter from the event organizer. When you accept the speaking engagement tell the organizer that, assuming they like your speech, you would like a testimonial letter. Most event organizers will be happy to provide one. (See the "preparing an information package" part of section 6.3 for more details about getting extraordinary testimonial letters – the kind that can convince employers to hire you.)

Another type of testimonial is comments from people who have heard you speak. You can include them as quotations in the letters you send to potential employers. Here is one of mine:

> *"Valuable, humorous and very motivating. 'Chock full' of hints and pearls of wisdom that will save me time, effort and frustration."*
>
> — L. Purdy, Department of National Defence, Calgary

To get testimonials, simply distribute a form at the end of your speech to ask for feedback. Your form should ask for the person's name and company. While anonymous evaluations may be useful when you are looking for honest feedback to improve your speaking skills, anonymous testimonials are not a good idea because people may think you made them up!

Finally, ask for permission to use the feedback. You can include a check box and a statement like "Please check here if we may quote you." You may be surprised how many people are happy to give testimonials to a good speaker.

With testimonials, not only will you be able to tell potential employers, "I have spoken on this topic numerous times," you will be able to supply proof of your speaking ability from "happy customers."

Evaluation forms can be an excellent source of leads themselves. If your audience includes prospective clients, you can ask for their contact information at the top of the form (address, phone number, e-mail address) and use the bottom of the form for marketing. For example, if you publish a newsletter, ask people if they want to subscribe.

You can also ask "Do you know other people or organizations that might be interested in a program like this?" then ask for their name, phone number and e-mail address.

Sample Speaker Evaluation for Testimonials

Your Name: _____ Title: _____

Company: _____

1. Which parts of the program were most valuable to you?

2. What else would you like to see included in this program?

3. What was your overall opinion of the program and speaker?

❑ Please check here if we may quote you

Promoting Yourself During the Speech

Whenever you have the opportunity to do a speech, let your audience know you are available for other speaking engagements. Some ways to do this are:

- Have the person who introduces you say in the introduction that you are available for other speaking engagements.

- Distribute a handout that has your name and contact information printed on it. Make sure the handout has valuable information so that audience members will hang on to it.

- End your speech on a high, with the audience wanting more. Then remind the audience that you are available to speak to other groups.

- Bring plenty of business cards to hand out, and be available to speak with audience members before and after your speech.

Once you begin actively promoting yourself, you will likely start to hear from prospective clients. However, beware if you get a call "out of the blue" from someone asking for a proposal.

6.6 Preparing Proposals

Occasionally you may be asked by an employer to submit a "proposal" to do some speaking work. A proposal is a written document, usually in the form of a letter, outlining what you propose to do for an organization. (Details about the contents of a proposal are in section 7.4.3.)

As mentioned, sometimes the request for a proposal may come "out of the blue" from an employer you haven't approached. The beginning speaker typically thinks this is great news! After all, why would they ask for a proposal if they were not interested? Actually, there are a number of reasons employers ask for proposals:

It May Be Necessary for the Job

In some cases, a proposal is necessary for the job. For example, many government departments require the decision-maker to review written proposals from several different prospects before a contract is awarded. They will often have formal RFP (request for proposal) guidelines for you to follow.

Likewise, if you have an idea for a continuing education course you would like to teach, most continuing education organizations will ask for a written proposal. The person you speak with should be able to tell you what they need in your proposal to make their decision.

If you pay attention to how they communicate with you, you should also get a sense of how your proposal will be treated when it is received. Are they encouraging? Do they return your calls promptly? Do they sound positive about your chances? If the answer to these questions is "yes" and you want the job, it is probably worth your time to write the proposal. This is the exception to the rule. In most cases, writing a proposal will be a waste of your time and energy.

It May Be a "Brush Off"

Some employers find it difficult to say "no" and want to avoid a confrontation. They can delay saying no by having you submit a proposal. The employer can then say it is "under review" (I saw this go on with one speaker for more than a year) until you either give up or they finally work up the courage to tell you they are not interested.

It May Be Used to Confirm a Hiring Decision

The most common reason some employers ask for proposals is because they want to have written comparisons of several speakers. Often, they have a "preferred" speaker in mind, and the purpose of the written proposals is to help them confirm their decision, or show their supervisor or a hiring committee that they have "shopped around."

> **TIP:** If you are the preferred speaker you will know it. The employer will have discussed the position with you in detail, and you will have reached a tentative agreement to do the work. They will explain that their regulations require them to review written proposals and may even assure you that it will be "just a formality."

If you are the preferred speaker and you want the job, then it is worth your time to put together a proposal confirming the details you have discussed with the employer. Otherwise, you could be wasting your time. Your time could be better spent focusing on employers who are seriously interested in you.

As you read in section 6.5, an employer who approaches you will not generally start off by asking for a proposal if they are seriously interested in working with you. If they do need more information, they will usually want to discuss it first.

If you suspect that a prospective employer is not serious, but don't want to miss out on what could potentially be a good opportunity, you might try what some other speakers and trainers do when asked for a proposal. They charge a "proposal preparation fee" which is deductible from their speaking fee if they get the job. Here is an example of what you can say about a proposal preparation fee:

> We are able to keep our fees low because we focus on speaking, not proposal-writing. If you are currently exploring several options and would like a written proposal from us, the fee is $250 which is deductible from the cost of future speaking.

For advice on writing a proposal see section 7.4.3.

6.7 Rates of Pay

A speaker's pay can range from "a coffee mug and a handshake" to $150,000. Most speakers fall somewhere in between. (Although I do have a lovely collection of coffee mugs from non-profit groups I have spoken for.)

When you are starting out, you may find that the organizations that ask you to speak will tell you what they are offering to pay. For example, if an organization has a speaker budget of only a few hundred dollars, they will usually say so up front.

However, these are the exceptions to the rule. As a motivational speaker, you are the one who decides what your fees will be. Many employers will ask "What are your fees?" when you discuss working together. If you are asked this question you need to have an answer.

If you don't have an answer, or say "it's negotiable," you will not sound like a professional. Professional speakers have "fee schedules" that they provide on request to prospective clients (although some speakers are willing to negotiate their published fees). A fee schedule is a published list of fees for different lengths of speaking engagements. Most speakers have a fee for:

- a keynote presentation (up to 90 minutes in length)

- a half day presentation

- a full day presentation

The fee schedule may also include fees for other services such as consultations.

Setting Your Fees

Speakers charge a wide range of fees. When determining your own fees, the primary factor to consider is the demand for your services. If you are only being invited to do free talks, you may not be ready to charge a fee. However, if someone approaches you after one of those free talks, says they are interested in hiring you, and asks what you charge, you are ready to charge a fee.

A beginner who speaks to schools might start at $200 and raise the price as they get more bookings. On the other hand, a beginner with professional materials (a professional video and full-color print materials) who is booked to speak at conferences might start at $1,000 per keynote.

Sample Fee Schedule

- Keynote (up to 90 minutes) $1,000

- Half day seminar (up to 3 hours) $1,500

- Full day seminar (up to 6 hours) $2,000

Outside of (your city) add airfare, hotel, and expenses.

Most speakers charge higher fees for longer programs. However, some speakers actually charge more for a keynote than they do for a full day. Your own fees might be based on such factors as:

- how much in demand your services are

- how much you want to earn

- what your expenses are, including whether you have to pay a commission to a speakers bureau

- what your competitors charge

Generally, a lower fee will result in more work, and it is time to raise your fees when you have more work than you can handle, or if you want to work less. In some cases, raising fees may help you get work by signalling to employers that you are an experienced professional. (An employer may associate low fees with little experience.)

While a few speakers believe it is not a good idea to negotiate fees, others will reduce their fee in return for benefits (such as a free cruise), additional bookings (e.g. a 25% discount for two or more programs booked at the same time), or simply if it will help them to get the job. Many speakers also charge a lower fee to speak to non-profit groups.

Your own fee schedule may be as simple as the one above, or you may want to include other services such as: consultations (an hourly fee), recording rights (mentioned earlier in this chapter), newsletter articles, or other activities (the next chapter has a list of services speakers are hired to provide at conferences).

Travel Expenses

The client typically pays for all travel expenses, including air fare, hotel, meals, and local transportation. Some speakers ask that the client make the travel arrangements and pay those expenses directly. However, the speaker is usually expected to make their own arrangements, pay those expenses, then be reimbursed.

To avoid having clients feel like they are being "nickeled and dimed," some speakers will charge a "per diem" (per day) fee of perhaps $50 to cover out-of-pocket expenses such as meals and local transportation instead of submitting every invoice. Others cover their own travel costs and charge different fees for local and non-local speaking engagements. For example, a local keynote might cost $1,000, but a keynote more than 100 miles outside of your city might cost $2,000.

7. Types of Employers

In the pages that follow, you will read about various employers that hire speakers. Each section describes what these employers are looking for, where to find contact information, and how to improve your odds of getting hired.

One question that comes up repeatedly when I teach my seminars for speakers is, "What's the best way for a beginner to break into the speaking business?" That question is answered in the next section.

7.1 Best Ways for Beginners to Break In

There are several ways that someone with no previous experience can start working as a professional speaker. These include:

Teach Continuing Education Classes

Many continuing education programs are constantly on the lookout for new part-time teachers to replace departing teachers. They are usually more concerned with the instructor's skills or life experience than their educational background.

After reading section 2.1, you should have a long list of your own skills and life experience. You can read more about continuing education programs in section 7.5.

Present Speeches and Seminars

One of the best ways for beginners to break in is to do something known in the speaking business as "going from free to fee." Even a few unpaid speaking engagements could give you the experience and references you need to start earning money as a speaker at conferences, schools, or colleges. See section 6.5.6 for more information.

You don't even have to get booked for free speeches to start getting experience. You can "hire yourself" by presenting your own seminars on any topic of your choice. Depending on the topic, your own seminars could give you the experience you need to start doing freelance training and speaking for corporations, government departments, and non-profit organizations. Section 9.5 explains how to put on your own seminars.

In the sections that follow you will discover some additional tips to help you get hired by specific types of employers.

7.2 Conventions, Conferences, Meetings, and Trade Shows

Every year thousands of speakers are hired to speak at conventions, conferences, meetings, and trade shows. The people who hire speakers for many of these events usually have the title of "meeting planner."

There are a variety of other titles for the individuals and groups that hire speakers, such as "conference organizer," "event planner," "speaker coordinator," or "convention committee."

7.2.1 Speaking Opportunities

Convention, Conference, and Meeting Opportunities

A convention is a formal meeting of members of an association. Any group of people with a common interest may form an association. For example, there are professional associations of doctors, lawyers, managers, administrative assistants, public relations professionals, and many other occupations. Likewise, there are industry associations for people who work in particular industries, such as banking, fashion, construction, travel, insurance, and many others.

Among the thousands of associations are local, state and provincial, national and international groups. Many of these groups hold an annual convention (which may be called an "annual meeting" or "conference") that they hire speakers for. There are speaking opportunities even with groups you probably have never heard of. For example, my first paid speaking engagement was delivering the keynote speech for an annual meeting of the Association of Gerontological Nurses of Alberta.

While a smaller event may have only one paid keynoter, a large convention that runs for several days may use more than 100 paid speakers. Following are some of the opportunities at a large convention:

- Keynote speaker

- Speakers for each meal (breakfast, lunch, and dinner)

- Master of Ceremonies

- Workshop leaders

- Facilitators for breakout sessions (sessions on a number of different topics, held simultaneously).

- Participating in a panel discussion

- Speakers for partner programs (may also be called "companion programs" or "spouse programs"). These programs offer topics of interest to people attending with those who have registered for the convention.

In addition to their annual meeting, or convention, some groups hold meetings and hire speakers for a number of events throughout the year. The person who books speakers for association events may be a member of the executive board with the title "speaker coordinator."

Trade Show Opportunities

Another type of event that speakers may be hired for is a trade show (may also be called an "expo" or "exhibition"). A trade show features a display of booths promoting products and services of interest to the people attending the show. Some trade shows are aimed at members of a particular industry.

Other shows are aimed at consumers. These events are often widely advertised to the public, and focus on a specific theme such as autos, gardening, bridal, business opportunities, or other topics of interest to consumers.

While the speakers at some trade shows are unpaid (these are usually industry personnel or exhibitors), other trade shows hire speakers to help draw more people to attend. A trade show may feature a paid keynote speaker, along with speakers for workshops or seminars throughout the day.

7.2.2   What These Employers Want

For small events with low budgets, the organizer may simply try to find a local expert who can provide some useful information to the association's members. For large events, employers expect more.

One of the most important considerations of people who hire speakers for conventions, conferences, or trade shows is finding speakers who will help to draw a crowd. The success of these events is usually measured, to some extent, by how many people attend. This is one reason why celebrities are often hired to speak at large conventions. More people will register if a celebrity is on the agenda.

Meeting planners also want speakers who will make them look good. This happens when audience members:

- Are glad they attended

- Feel they have received more than their money's worth

- Want to attend future events

Meeting planners know from experience that the speakers who make the audience feel this way tend to be extremely dynamic, entertaining professionals. These qualities may not be as important for small local events, but they can certainly help to get any speaking job.

7.2.3   How to Improve Your Odds of Getting Hired

Here are some things you can do to help you get hired to speak at conventions, conferences, meetings, and trade shows:

Show Them You Can Draw a Crowd

To convince a meeting planner you can help them to draw a large crowd, show them evidence of your past speeches that had high attendance. (A video demo of you speaking in front of a huge audience is a start.)

Offer to Help Get Media Coverage

Many organizations want media coverage for their event, so you should emphasize the popularity of your topic with the media. Show them that you have been able to get media coverage in the past by including article clippings or a list of media interviews in your information package. You could also offer to do telephone interviews with the media before the event or offer to come a day early to do TV interviews.

Make Your Name Known

Get your name in front of meeting planners at every opportunity using the self-promotion techniques described in section 6.5. If the meeting planner has heard of you they are more likely to assume you will help draw a crowd and make them look good. Remember to keep in touch with many meeting planners because, although most associations use different keynote speakers every year, a good speaker may be invited back a few years later.

Get Testimonials

If a meeting planner hasn't heard of you, you can help show them you are a professional by getting testimonials from other meeting planners. It also helps to include a client list in your information package provided some of the company names on that list are well known.

Work With Speakers Bureaus

Many meeting planners rely on speakers bureaus for recommendations of speakers. Use the information in chapter 8 to establish relationships with some bureaus.

Help Them Make Money From Your Talk

Many local associations that can afford to hire speakers for their annual conventions may not have the funds to pay speakers at other times of the year. What you can offer to do is help organize a fundraising event from which you split the profits.

More details on organizing this type of event can be found in section 7.4.5.

7.2.4   How to Find Out About Upcoming Events

There are several websites that provide lists of upcoming events that may need speakers. These sites let you search for events by industry, type of event, and location. For most events, you can then click on a link to find out contact information.

To find out about upcoming events, visit **www.allconferences.net**, **www.tradeshows.com**, and the Trade Show Exhibitors Association site at **www.tsea.org**.

Hundreds of conference speaking opportunities are listed online at SpeakerMatch. Subscribers have access to information about 30-50 events that need speakers every month. While many of these are non-paying, about 30% pay a speaking fee of $500 or more. Subscriptions start at $49.95 per month. Visit **www.speakermatch.com** for details.

7.2.5   Association Contact Information

The website for the American Society of Association Executives has links to over 6,500 associations. You can search for associations at the ASAE's website by going to **www.asaecenter.org**. (Click on "People & Groups" then on "Find a Member" then look for the "Gateway to Associations" link.)

When you visit an association website, search for the name and e-mail address of a contact person. Send a brief e-mail to that person asking who hires speakers for conventions and other events. Many of the people you contact should either e-mail you an answer or forward your e-mail to the right person.

Another good source of association information is the annual publication *National Trade and Professional Associations of the United States* (NTPA), published by Columbia Books. It lists thousands of associations along with their address, telephone, and fax number. Many e-mail and web addresses are also included, along with a contact person – either the president, executive director or an administrator of the group. For larger organizations, an additional contact for meetings and conventions is listed. The NTPA is available for $299. You can order it from **www. columbiabooks.com** or by calling (888) 265-0600.

You can find a list of some Canadian Professional Associations at **www. charityvillage.com/cv/nonpr/index.asp**.

7.2.6   Network With Employers

If you want to network with meeting planners, there are a number of organizations you could join. As section 6.5.5 explained, for the best results it is recommended that you become actively involved in any group you join.

Membership in organizations such as the American Society of Association Executives, Meeting Professionals International, or the Professional Convention Management Association typically costs several hundred dollars. Speakers are allowed to join these organizations as "Associate Members" or "Suppliers."

American Society of Association Executives

Phone: (202) 371-0940
Website: **www.asaecenter.org**
Cost: $395 U.S. per year (Consultant)

Meeting Professionals International

Phone: (972) 702-3000
Website: **www.mpiweb.org**
Cost: $375 U.S./$425 Cdn. per year (Supplier Membership)

Professional Convention Management Association

Phone: (312) 423-7262
Website: **www.pcma.org**
Cost: $475 U.S. per year (Supplier Partner Membership)

It's a good idea to network with the staff of your local convention and visitors bureau, and the sales staff at major hotels, because they can refer business to you. Associations often ask these people to recommend local speakers. Show them what you can do. Send them your materials and ask to make a brief presentation (under 10 minutes) at the next meeting of their sales staff.

7.3 Seminar and Training Companies

There are two significant areas of employment with seminar and training companies:

In-house Programs

In-house programs (also known as onsite programs) are presented for personnel of one particular organization.

Public Seminars

Public seminars are programs that are open to the public. The people who attend may have been sent by their companies, or they may have paid the registration fee themselves.

7.3.1 Opportunities With National Companies

One of the advantages of working with a national company is that you do not have to develop your own programs. Most companies provide the seminar content, and you simply add some personal stories.

Although seminar companies are typically known for offering public seminars, and training companies usually focus on onsite programs, most seminar and training companies actually offer both types of programs. In fact, the job title both types of companies may use for someone who presents programs is "trainer."

Some national companies hire trainers to present both public seminars and onsite programs in cities across North America or around the world. Once you have made it through the hiring process, you will be given a work schedule that may require you to travel to as many as five different cities in a single week. (All travel expenses are paid by the company.)

The number of seminars you would be scheduled to present in a particular month depends on a variety of factors including the particular employer, the topics you can present, your availability, and your performance in previous months. You could end up working either full-time or part-time.

Other companies hire trainers on a contract basis for onsite and public programs in the trainer's own city. These companies may hire trainers on an "as-needed" basis. In other words, when the company has a client that wants a particular program you can present, you may be hired for the job. This means that even if a company decides to make you one of its trainers, you may work for them only a few days per year.

Companies Actively Seeking Trainers

There are a number of seminar companies that hire on an ongoing basis. Most companies have a formal application procedure, although what they are looking for varies from one company to another. In many cases, you will need to fill out an application and submit a video demo.

The company may then invite you to an audition in your own city or another city (travel may be either at your own expense or the company's expense), where you would do a presentation in front of a panel.

The following companies hire trainers based in the United States, and many hire Canadian trainers as well. You can find details about their opportunities and how to apply through their websites:

American Management Association

Address: 1601 Broadway
New York, NY 10019

Phone: (877) 566-9441

Website: **www.amanet.org/faculty/who_we_are.htm**

Canadian Management Centre

Address: 150 York Street, 5th Floor
Toronto, ON M5H 3S5

Phone: (877) 262-2500

Website: **www.cmcamai.org/reg/course_leaders_info.html**

Fred Pryor Seminars/CareerTrack

Address: Trainer Review Committee
9757 Metcalf Avenue
Overland Park, KS 66212

Phone: (800) 780-8476

Website: **www.pryor.com/career/seminar_leader.asp**

National Center for Continuing Education

Address: Attention: Joseph Weil
967 Briarcliff Drive
Tallahassee, FL 32308

Fax: (850) 222-4862

Email: jw@nccetraining.com

Website: **www.nccetraining.com/recruit.cfm**

Padgett-Thompson/National Seminars Group

Address: Rockhurst University Continuing Education Center
P.O. Box 419107
Kansas City, MO 64141-6107

Phone: (800) 258-7246

Website: **www.nationalseminarstraining.com/careeropps/
careeropps.html**

SkillPath Seminars

Address: 6900 Squibb Road
P.O. Box 2768
Mission, KS 66201-2768

Phone: (800) 873-7545

Email: recruit@skillpath.net

Website: **www.skillpath.com/careers**

7.3.2   Local Seminar and Training Companies

There are dozens of local seminar and training companies in every major city. While a few of these companies hire trainers, most are small businesses struggling to find enough training work for the companies' owners.

A typical local company has one or two owners who started the business because they love speaking and training. Running their own business means they may also have to do a lot of work they don't love – such as bookkeeping, office administration, advertising, cold calling, seminar organizing, and other tasks. However, they do this work because it allows them the opportunity to do what they really want to do – speak in front of a group.

> **NOTE:**   With most small companies, when you apply to be a trainer you are essentially asking the company owners to do more of the work they don't love, and offering to take away some of the work they do love.

This is certainly not true of all local seminar and training companies, but it is true of enough of them that it is usually not worth investing too much time applying to these companies. However, as you will read below under "Improve Your Odds of Getting Hired," it is possible to get hired even by a small local company if you approach them the right way.

You can find local companies listed in the Yellow Pages under "training" or "management consultants."

7.3.3   What These Employers Want

Excellent Delivery

Every seminar company expects its presenters to have outstanding speaking skills.

Business Experience

The main source of income for most seminar and training companies is business programs. This means that most seminar companies are seeking people who can effectively teach programs on such topics as customer service, financial management, sales, project management, supervisory skills, and other business-related topics. ("Personal growth seminars" are covered at the end of this section.)

As a result, most companies want trainers who have business experience in the topic they will be teaching. The amount of experience required varies from zero to 10 years, depending on the company.

Sales Ability

A significant source of income for seminar and training companies is "back of the room" (BOR) product sales. If you have ever attended a public seminar, you may remember that before each break participants are urged to rush to the back of the room to buy resource products like tapes, videos, and books. Trainers who can sell a significant amount make more money and get hired to present more programs.

7.3.4   How to Improve Your Odds of Getting Hired

Get a Great Video Demo

To be seriously considered by most seminar companies, you will need to submit an outstanding video demo. (Although a few companies don't require a demo, having one could give you an edge over applicants who don't.) Your video does not have to be professional quality, but it should show you as a dynamic, professional-looking presenter who can interact effectively with participants. See section 6.4 for details about how to prepare a video demo.

Do an Outstanding Audition

For your audition, prepare a 15-20 minute presentation (it may be longer or shorter depending on the instructions the seminar company gives you) of your best material.

- It should be on a topic the seminar company offers (e.g. no speaking on pet grooming for a business seminar company!)

- It should be both informative and entertaining. Include some excellent advice plus at least one personal story or anecdote.

- Dress as you would if you were actually teaching the seminar. You can see examples of how speakers dress at their websites. For my successful audition with the American Management Association, I wore a navy blue suit with a gold high necked blouse, small gold accessories, low heeled navy pumps, and neutral pantyhose. (The audition was held in San Francisco, but I wore similar outfits during their all expenses paid speaker training in New York City.)

- Bring copies of your information package and business cards.

- Smile and be friendly with everyone you encounter at the audition site, including the receptionist and cleaning staff. You are being judged on how you will be to work with.

- Be prepared to answer questions and do some impromptu speaking on a topic they give you at the audition. (Ask in advance what to expect.)

- Follow up with thank you letters.

Apply to Companies That Are Actively Recruiting

It may sound obvious, but it is worth saying: companies that are actively recruiting will be more likely to respond positively to an application. So start your job search with the companies listed above under "Companies Actively Seeking Trainers."

You can still apply to companies that are not actively recruiting using the techniques described in chapter 6 of this guide, but you may need to work harder to land a job.

Use the Right Job Title

As mentioned at the beginning of this section, a standard job title for someone who presents programs for seminar or training companies is "trainer." Other job titles include:

- course leader

- instructor

- faculty member

- seminar leader

The job title "speaker" is rarely used by seminar and training companies. That's because among many business decision-makers, there is a perception that a "speaker" is someone with good delivery but only superficial content, while a "trainer" is more likely to have both good delivery and in-depth content.

When companies send employees to a full-day program, they don't just want them to spend the day hearing inspiring messages, they want their employees to spend the day learning practical techniques to help them improve particular skills.

> **TIP:** When you approach seminar and training companies, don't describe yourself as a "speaker." Instead, describe yourself as a "trainer" or whatever job title they use.

Prove Your Value to Potential Employers

Virtually all employers want to know that you will bring them more value than you cost. You can do this with national seminar and training companies by providing evidence that you delight audiences and sell large volumes of BOR (back of room) products.

So how do you provide this evidence if you have never been hired as a trainer? The answer is to present your own seminars as explained in section 9.5. Whether you invite them to come see you in action or put together a video demo from seminar clips, you show that you can draw an audience and keep them entertained.

With local seminar and training companies, you can show your value in other ways.

> **EXAMPLE:**
> I was able to convince a small local seminar company to offer my program on "Publish Your Book – From the Idea to the Bookstore" by explaining to the company owner that my seminar would make his company a healthy profit in return for minimal effort on his part. Before approaching him, I had presented the program as a continuing education course which was easy to market and sold out every time it was offered.

Facilitating Personal Growth Seminars

If you have ever taken a "personal growth" seminar, you know how powerful these programs can be. During these multi-day programs, participants may learn new insights about themselves, develop skills for achieving better results in life, and grow both emotionally and spiritually. These programs may be intense and profound, with participants sharing their thoughts and feelings more openly than they ever have before.

Participating in a well-run personal growth seminar can be an awesome experience. It is no wonder that a significant number of participants (as many as 10-20 percent, according to one source) decide that they would like to become facilitators, so they can lead others through what they have experienced.

You can find organizations offering personal growth seminars in virtually every major city. If you do a search for "personal growth" at YellowPages.com for the state of Texas, for example, you may find such entries as the "Personal Growth and Development Center," "New Visions Center for Personal Growth," and "Life Concepts for Personal Growth." Of course, there are many similar companies that do not actually use the words "personal growth" in their names.

Each company that hires personal growth facilitators has its own application process. To be considered, applicants must typically complete all levels of the organization's personal growth seminars. They must then be accepted into a facilitator training program.

The cost to take all of these programs can run into thousands of dollars, and there are usually far more graduates of each organization's facilitator training programs than the organization can hire. While this may be an ideal career path for a few, for most would-be facilitators it is easier and more profitable to present your own seminars.

See section 9.5 for information on how to present your own seminars.

7.4 Corporations, Government Agencies, and Non-Profit Organizations

7.4.1 Types of Opportunities

Corporations, government agencies, and non-profit organizations hire speakers for events such as conferences, conventions, or meetings. Many of these opportunities for speakers are covered in section 7.2. An additional opportunity, speaking at non-profit fund-raisers, is covered at the end of this section.

In addition to speaking opportunities, organizations offer a number of opportunities for contract "trainers." While this goes beyond speaking, it is included here because many speakers supplement their income by presenting training programs.

What is a Contract Trainer?

Contract trainers are self-employed individuals who provide training services to companies, government agencies, or non-profit organizations. While most trainers work for a variety of different clients, some find that most of their work is done for one particular client organization.

Types of Training

Trainers may present training programs in a variety of areas:

Job Training

These programs teach employees specific skills they will need on the job. Employees may learn how to use equipment, work with particular computer programs, assemble products, and other essential job skills. A significant amount of training is done for employees who deal with the public. As a result, some trainers specialize in sales training or customer service training.

If a job is potentially dangerous, employees will also receive safety training, such as how to handle hazardous materials and administer first aid.

Professional Development

This type of training covers a variety of skills that, while they may not be an essential part of the job, can help employees to do their jobs more effectively. Topics include: time management, communication skills, negotiating techniques, assertiveness training, stress management, business writing, and critical thinking.

Supervisory and Management Skills

These programs are presented to people who supervise or manage employees. Among the topics that may be taught are delegation, motivation, coaching, conflict resolution, team building, performance evaluation, diversity, and project management.

Executive Development

These are programs for senior executives on topics such as leadership, strategic planning, and media relations.

Duties of a Trainer

As a trainer you might carry out a variety of activities in addition to speaking, including:

Needs Assessment

This involves identifying the training needs of the organization. To find out whether employee training is needed, for example, you would conduct research to determine if there is a gap between desired employee performance and actual performance. This research might include meeting with company executives and managers. You would then determine whether training might help solve the problem by improving employee skills, knowledge, or attitudes.

Program Design

Once the need for training has been established, you may be responsible for designing the training program. This process is also known by such terms as "instructional design" and "curriculum development." To design training programs you will need a solid knowledge of adult learning theory, covered later in this section.

In addition to writing the material that the trainer will deliver, you would design group exercises and prepare instructional materials.

Training Delivery

This involves conducting training sessions through such methods as presenting information, facilitating group discussions, and directing participants through exercises or the use of interactive multimedia. The training may take place with participants in a classroom, or it might be conducted on-the-job. Another option is train-the-trainer sessions which teach employees how to train their co-workers.

7.4.2   What These Employers Want

The people who hire trainers usually prefer to hire candidates with previous experience in instructional design and training delivery. The next section of this guide has ideas to help you develop the traits that employers want.

Knowledge of Adult Learning Theory

Organizations expect their trainers to understand how to teach adults. If you are familiar with "adult learning theory" (how adults learn) you can develop training programs that adults will find both engaging and educational.

One principle of teaching adults is that lecturing is not an effective way of teaching most subjects. Instead, adults prefer to learn by doing. As a result, effective trainers typically have trainees participate in a variety of activities such as group discussions, role plays, brainstorming, games, completing questionnaires, and watching videos.

However, avoid having too many games in a training session or you risk having participants feel the training is a waste of time. This is be-cause of another important principle of adult learning theory – adult learners need to be shown why something is relevant. As a trainer, you will need to explain how the material you are teaching can be applied to their work. To illustrate, which of the following do you think would be the most effective exercise for an employee training session on con-flict resolution?

Exercise #1:

Participants break into groups of three. You then give them a make-believe scenario about a conflict between a teenager who has been skipping classes and her parents. Participants discuss and try to resolve the situation by "role playing" (acting) the parts of the teenager and parents.

Exercise #2:

You ask participants to think of a situation where they personally have experienced conflict. They then break into pairs and you give them several questions so they can discuss what they experienced. For those who prefer not to discuss a personal situation, you can suggest they discuss a conflict they have observed. As part of the discussion, or as a separate activity, you have participants role play what they would say if they experienced a similar situation in future.

In the first exercise, participants are unlikely to see any direct application to their work. In the second exercise, participants can discuss and find ways of dealing with situations they have actually experienced or are likely to experience in the future.

You can learn techniques for teaching adults through continuing education classes and organizations such as the American Society for Training and Development at **www.astd.org**. There are also many books available with training exercises, such as the popular series *Games Trainers Play*, by John W. Newstrom and Edward E. Scannell.

If you don't want to create your own training programs, you can buy programs that have already been developed on subjects such as communications, change, creativity, customer relations, diversity, leadership, management, sales, stress management, teamwork, and other topics.

For example, Inscape Publishing offers Facilitator's Kits containing a fully-scripted seminar, and transparency masters and reproducible handouts. Facilitators Kits cost $600, and can be purchased through a distributor such as Rebecca Morgan at **www.rebeccamorgan.com/carlson.html**.

Analytical Skills

As mentioned under "Duties of a Trainer," trainers are expected to be able to perform tasks such as needs assessments and program evaluations. To do so, you must be able to ask the right questions, and analyze the answers.

When you are doing a needs assessment, the types of questions you might ask are:

- Who is this training for?

- What kind of training programs have they had in the past? Were those programs effective or not? Why?

- Why do you want to hold the current training?

- What are the specific problems you want solved?

- What specific topics do you want to be covered?

- What are the results you expect from this training?

- What do you need to be satisfied with the training?

- What do the participants want from attending this program?

- Is there anything else you think I need to know?

- Do company practices support this training?

The final question can help give realistic expectations for the training. For example, if you are being asked to train customer service representatives to give more personal attention to customers, but the company awards bonuses based on how quickly customer calls are handled, the training is unlikely to achieve its objective.

After the training, your evaluation might be done through methods such as: evaluation forms (both immediately after the training and a month later), interviewing trainees or their supervisors, asking customers, and measuring results.

For example, if you held a training program with the aim of reducing complaints about the company's customer service, you could measure the number of complaints both before and after the training. Of course, to do a good analysis you would need to examine other factors besides the training that might have affected the number of complaints.

Communication Skills

Trainers need to excel in a variety of communication skills including:

- Interpersonal skills (for working with managers to develop training)

- Written communication skills (for preparing reports)

- Presentation skills

7.4.3   How to Improve Your Odds of Getting Hired

Get Experience

An excellent way to get training experience before you approach employers is to present your own seminars on business related topics. Section 9.5 has information on how to present your own seminars.

You can get instructional design experience through a variety of educational programs as described below.

Get an Education

Many organizations prefer to work with trainers who have degrees in the subject they are teaching, or in an area such as human resources, education, or training and development. If you would like to earn a degree quickly, section 6.5 has information about alternative degree programs.

Other educational options include taking a certificate program, online courses, continuing education classes, or professional development seminars through a college or organization such as the American Society for Training and Development (ASTD).

Learn to "Talk the Talk"

To appear to be a competent trainer, it helps to speak the language. Of course this includes referring to yourself as "a trainer" and not "a speaker," but it goes further. When you apply for a training job you may hear terms like "accelerated learning," "experiential," "best practices," and acronyms like "ROI" (return on investment), "CBT" (computer based training), "WBT" (web based training), "HPI" (human performance improvement), and "SME" (subject matter expert). If you don't understand what the employer is talking about it can definitely hurt your chances of getting the job.

One way to learn the lingo is through involvement in the American Society for Training and Development. Annual membership costs $180 and includes a subscription to *Training & Development* magazine and online access to *Human Resource Development Quarterly*. You can even pick up some lingo just browsing their website at **www.astd.org/astd**.

Go Directly to the People Who Can Hire You

While the human resources department often contracts with trainers, it is a good idea to also approach decision-makers in the appropriate departments because they may have the authority to hire you. If you offer sales training, you could also contact the vice president of sales, sales directors, and sales managers throughout the organization. (Techniques for contacting potential employers are described in detail in section 6.3.)

Realize that it may take months to break into a particular organization. Contacting as many decision-makers as possible within that organization can help improve your odds of getting hired more quickly.

Learn to Write Proposals

As section 6.6 explains, writing proposals can be a waste of time with many potential employers. However, in most cases you simply cannot get a government contract unless you write a proposal, as detailed below.

As a potential "supplier" of training services to government, you would receive a Request for Proposal or RFP. (To be invited to submit a proposal, you will first have to ensure government departments and agencies are aware of your services, using some of the techniques described in chapter 6.) When you submit your proposal, you are making a "bid" to do the work.

A typical RFP is a document that provides information about the organization, their training needs, the target audience, what they require in a proposal, and instructions for submission of the proposal. Here is an example of the type of information expected in a proposal:

- A description of your training company

- Demonstration of your capability to develop and deliver the program

- Detailed description of the approach you will take in the training

- A proposed timetable

- A fixed price quotation for development and delivery of the program

- Specific resources (such as trainers) that you will assign to the project

- References from organizations you've done similar programs for

- An explanation of how you will measure results of the training

The bid process may also require you to make an oral presentation. The client may not be obligated to award the contract to the "lowest cost" bidder. Instead, they may make their decision based on a number of factors, including the training company's previous experience presenting similar training.

A number of companies specialize in writing proposals. You can find them by doing a web search for "writing proposals" and "contract." An excellent resource is Deborah Kluge's webpage with links on proposal writing and government contracting. Her proposal pointers are great! Visit **www.proposalwriter.com/links.html** to see for yourself.

Recommended books on proposal writing include *Proven Proposal Strategies to Win More Business,* by Herman Holtz, and *Win Government Contracts for Your Small Business,* by John Di Giacomo and James Kleckner.

7.4.4   Potential Employers

Most organizations do training of some kind, so they may be potential employers of contract trainers. Here are some ways to find information about different organizations.

Network With Potential Employers

It's a great idea to become a member of the American Society for Training and Development. ASTD has more than 150 local chapters which offer job referral services, along with regular meetings, newsletters, conferences and workshops, social activities, and other services. You can find local chapters in the "Membership" links on their website. You can contact ASTD at:

American Society for Training and Development

Address: 1640 King Street
Box 1443
Alexandria, VA 22313-2043

Phone: (703) 683-8100

Website: **www.astd.org**

Another good networking group is the Society for Human Resources Management (SHRM). There are more than 500 chapters that provide networking opportunities. A number of SHRM chapters also have online "job banks" listing local career opportunities in human resources. Contact them at:

Society for Human Resources Management

Address: 1800 Duke Street
Alexandria, VA 22314

Phone: (800) 283-7476 or (703) 548-3440

Website: **www.shrm.org**

You can find Canadian human resources organizations through the Canadian Council of Human Resources Associations at **www.chrpcanada. com**. If you specialize in a particular industry you should also network within that industry. For example, a sales trainer could join professional sales associations.

You can find associations within your industry by visiting the websites listed in section 7.2.

Directories

Your public library will have numerous directories with lists of companies, government departments, and non-profit organizations. You can also find lists of these organizations online.

Corporations

Hoover's Online at **www. hoovers.com** allows you to search for major U.S. companies by name or industry. To search by industry, look under the "Browse Industries" tab. For Canadian companies go to the *Globe & Mail* site at **www.reportonbusiness.com/top1000**.

Government

To find U.S. government resources, you can go to **www.govspot.com**. Links to Canadian government departments can be found at **http://canada.gc.ca/howgoc/howind_e.html**.

Non-Profit Organizations

GuideStar at **www.guidestar.com** is a searchable online database of more than 1.7 million non-profit organizations in the United States. If you click on "Advanced Search" you can search by your city, state, and non-profit category (e.g. Arts, Environment, Health). CharityVillage has a similar database of Canadian non-profit organizations. Go to **www.charityvillage.com/cv/nonpr/index.asp** to check it out.

7.4.5   Rates of Pay

Many trainers charge by the day. Fees vary, but it is not unusual to charge several thousand dollars a day for a training program. My usual rate is $1,500 for a half day and $3,000 for a full day, plus $1,500 for development (if it is not a program I usually present). I know other trainers who charge from $500 to $7,000 per day. However, if an organization has a specific amount budgeted, and it's a topic I specialize in (meaning I won't have to do a lot of extra research), I may be flexible on the fee.

More information about fees can be found in section 6.7.

Getting Paid by Non-Profit Organizations

Although many trainers charge lower fees to non-profits, it helps to remember that "non-profit" does not necessarily mean "no money." Like any organization, many non-profits find a way to pay for rent, postage, printing, employee salaries and benefits, and many other expenses.

> **EXAMPLE:**
> I remember working with one speaker who was doing free one-hour presentations for an organization because she assumed they

couldn't afford to pay her. She later learned that other speakers were being paid $300 to do similar presentations for the same organization. The only reason she wasn't being paid was because she hadn't asked, so the organization was happy to let her volunteer her services.

If a charity tells you they would like you to do your program, but can't afford to pay you, you can decide if it is a cause to which you are willing to donate your services. Another option, if you are dealing with an organization that feels it has "no money" is to offer a way to help them make money. If you speak on a topic that can draw a large crowd, it may be ideal for a charity fund-raiser. By selling tickets to your talk, a non-profit group can pay you for your services and raise additional funds for their organization. It is truly a "win-win" arrangement.

When you approach an organization with this idea, you should emphasize the benefits of your program to them, and show them that it is an excellent low-risk fund-raising opportunity, and a valuable program for those attending.

You can propose this type of arrangement to any organization that wants to raise money – which means most non-profit organizations, including associations, charities, and churches. (Of course, your topic should be something of interest to the group.) In most organizations the person to contact with your proposal is the Executive Director.

To make your proposal as attractive to the organization as possible, you can offer to be paid a share of the money raised from ticket sales. What this means to the organization is that they will not risk having to pay your fee if the event is not a success. It also means you have the potential to earn more than your standard fee.

The percentage you can make will vary depending on the organization and the amount of effort involved in organizing the event. However, the generally accepted split is 50-50 after expenses. (Some speakers negotiate for 50 percent before expenses.) Usually, the organization is responsible for promoting the event, handling logistics, and collecting funds, while the speaker is responsible only for speaking. However, it is recommended that to ensure a successful event you provide any assistance you can, such as doing media interviews or writing a newsletter article.

7.5 Continuing Education

Continuing education programs are any educational programs that do not lead to a degree. If you have ever wondered who would hire you to speak about a topic such as basket weaving, handwriting analysis, or wine making, the answer may be "continuing education programs."

Continuing education programs are presented on most topics that people are interested in learning, such as: art, business, computers, crafts, drama, fitness, languages, music, outdoor activities, travel, philosophy, photography, writing, and many others. Programs are offered for adults, teens, children, and seniors.

The usual title for someone who presents continuing education programs is "instructor," not "speaker" or "trainer."

7.5.1 Potential Employers

There are thousands of organizations offering continuing education programs, ranging from one-day seminars to courses presented once a week for an entire semester. Virtually every college and university offers continuing education programs, and so do many city parks and recreation departments and YMCAs.

The departments that offer these programs for colleges and universities go by a number of different names including:

- Adult education

- Continuing education

- Continuing studies

- Extension

- Further education

There are several online directories which offer links to websites of colleges and universities. A directory of U.S. colleges and universities is leges and universities. A directory of U.S. colleges and universities is located at **www.utexas.edu/world/univ**. You can find a list of Canadian universities at **www.uwaterloo.ca/canu**. And you can find links to colleges in the U.S. and Canada at **www.mcli.dist.maricopa.edu/cc**.

Most of the links on the above websites go to the college or university's home page. From there you will need to search for the continuing education department (keep in mind that it may have one of the other names listed above). If you can't find the right link for a particular institution, send a quick e-mail to the site's webmaster asking how to reach the continuing education department.

For your local parks and recreation department, check the phone book under listings for your civic government or call directory assistance. To find your local YMCA, check the phone book.

The Learning Annex

Another organization that hires instructors is The Learning Annex, which is described in company literature as "an alternative adult-education organization offering short, inexpensive courses on personal growth, business and career opportunities, showbiz and media, health and healing, sports and fitness, spirituality, relationships, and high tech."

A variety of Learning Annex courses are offered in locations across the U.S. and Canada. You can find out more at **www.thelearningannex.com**. To find contact information at that website, go to the main page, then click on "About Us," then on "Contact Us."

7.5.2   What These Employers Want

Most decision-makers for continuing education departments are looking for programs that will be popular with the public, taught by instructors who are "experts." When it comes to establishing your expertise, your education is usually less important than your experience in a particular topic. As one organization put it, they are looking for instructors "with practical knowledge and experience."

Section 6.5 has some good ideas to help you establish your expertise in whatever topic you want to teach.

7.5.3   How to Improve Your Odds of Getting Hired

Suggest a New Course

Offering to teach an existing continuing education course is usually a waste of time. Most continuing education organizations are inundated with applications from people offering to teach their existing programs.

Many continuing education decision-makers find that whenever they publish a new course catalog, scores of would-be instructors call up saying, "Hey, I could teach one of your courses." The problem with this approach is that if a course is in the catalog, the continuing education program already has somebody to teach it. Until that instructor quits (getting fired is rare), no one else – no matter how well-qualified – is likely to have an opportunity to teach it.

Thus, the number one way to improve your odds of getting hired by this type of employer is to propose a new course.

Apply to More Than One Organization

While one organization may seem an "ideal" fit for your course, it is possible they already have enough instructors in that area, or the decision-maker may have a personal prejudice against your background or suggested topic.

> **EXAMPLE:**
> I applied several times without success to teach a public relations course for a local community college. Eventually, the local university hired me to teach the program the college wasn't interested in. I later learned that the person who hired public relations instructors for the college had automatically rejected my application because I did not have a designation from a group she was active in – a group that only 10 percent of public relations professionals belong to. If I had kept applying only to that college, I would never have had the opportunity to teach that course.

So consider applying to a variety of continuing education programs. If you are willing to travel, you can apply to programs outside your community as well. Most programs will not pay travel expenses, so if you want to instruct in other communities it's a good idea to propose short courses that can be offered over one or two days.

7.5.4   Rates of Pay

Continuing education programs typically pay by the classroom hour, or by the participant. Hourly fees are low, and may range from $10 to $50 per hour, with higher fees paid by universities. The "per partici-pant" fee may also be a low amount such as $15 per person.

Beware of a "per participant" arrangement unless you are given a mini-mum fee guarantee (or are willing to work cheap for some other rea-son, such as experience or publicity). My partner Clayton and I once traveled 500 miles at our own expense to present a one-day program for a continuing education department. Due to a low enrollment, we split a grand total of $375 Canadian for our efforts.

> **TIP:**   Continuing education programs can be a great way to break in to the speaking business. There is high turn-over among continuing education instructors because of low pay, so most programs are constantly looking for new instructors.

7.5.5   How to Apply

Review Catalogs

When you first contact continuing education programs, you can simply ask them to mail you a catalog or check out their catalog online. This will tell you what courses they currently offer so you can come up with ideas for new courses.

If they already offer a course you would like to teach, see if there is a different angle you can take. For example, if they offer a fitness program you would like to teach, perhaps you could gear it to a particular audi-ence such as teens or seniors.

Speak With a Decision-Maker

Before deciding which particular courses you would like to teach, it's a good idea to get more information about the organization's needs. As long as you know the general subject area (such as business, comput-ers, or travel), you can contact the organization and ask the receptionist to put you through to the person who hires continuing education in-structors in your subject area.

The decision-maker's title will probably be something like "program director," "program planner," or "program designer." When you speak with this decision-maker, who we'll call the program director, ask what you need to do to apply and when the application deadline is.

You can also ask the program director how they make their decision and whether there are any courses in your subject area that they are seeking instructors for.

> **EXAMPLE:**
> One of the continuing education programs in my community recently advertised that they were seeking instructors for doz-ens of courses requested by the community. Their "wish list" included such diverse topics as "In-line Skating," "e-commerce," "Christmas Crafts," "Medical Office Assistant Training," "Songwriting for Teens," and "Payroll Management."

If an organization is advertising for instructors, you may face some com-petition, so even if you apply to teach one of those courses, it is prob-ably a good idea to also propose an entirely new course of your own.

> **TIP:** The application deadline may be four to six months before you would actually begin teaching the course. This is so the course can be advertised in the organization's catalog.

If you plan to do a mass mailing to continuing education programs outside your community, you don't need to call them all. However, you should call several within your community to get an idea of what these decision-makers expect.

Submit Your Materials

Different continuing education organizations have different require-ments. Some may ask you to fill out an application form. Others may ask for a resume or curriculum vitae, with or without a course outline.

> **TIP:** If you want to be taken seriously as an expert, it is usually not a good idea to propose many different courses. You are likely to have better results if you propose only one course, or if you propose a few related courses within one subject area.

To make a great impression, you might include any of the following items in addition to what the program director asks for. However, if you do include "optional" items, make sure that the items the program director wants to see are easy to find. Some of the following are described in more detail in section 6.3.2:

- A presentation folder

- A cover letter explaining why the proposed course will be popular

- A biography focusing on your expertise in the proposed topic

- Testimonial letters

- Other items from your information package

- A video demo

- A course description

Course Description

The program director may specify a length for the course description that would appear in the organization's catalog. This should include some benefits to people who register. Here is an example:

Sample Course Description

Media Relations
In this course you will learn principles and skills for effective media relations. You will discover how the media determines what is newsworthy, learn practical techniques for promoting your organization through media publicity, and understand how to work with the media on an ongoing basis. The course covers print, broadcast, and online media relations.

Follow Up

After you have sent your package, you can call the program directors to ensure they have everything they need to make a decision. If your course is not selected for the next semester, you can stay in touch to let them know you are available for future semesters.

7.6   Schools and Colleges

If you want to make a difference in the lives of young people, one way to do so is by speaking at schools or colleges. There are opportunities to speak to students in elementary schools, middle schools, high schools, and colleges.

7.6.1   What These Employers Want

Topics That Are Most in Demand

While colleges and schools hire speakers on a variety of topics – from astronomy to communication skills – there is tremendous demand for motivational speakers. Motivational speakers are those who can inspire young people to make the right choices in life. They may help students learn how to overcome obstacles and achieve goals. Or they may specialize in "prevention" topics and speak about how to avoid drugs, gangs, crime, or sex.

Among the other topics schools hire speakers for are self-esteem, multicultural diversity, and leadership skills. Colleges are also interested in programs that offer advice on achieving success in college, or getting a job after college.

Speakers Who've "Been There, Done That"

The speakers who have the greatest impact on students are those who speak from personal experience. For example, it is far more powerful for students to hear about the dangers of gangs from a former gang member than from someone who has simply studied gangs.

An example of a speaker who relates to students is Jeff Yalden (**www.jeffyalden.com**). Yalden overcame several setbacks and a poor (**www.jeffyalden.com**). Yalden overcame several setbacks and a poor self-image and completely turned his life around. He now shares his experiences with teenagers who are struggling to "fit in."

Speakers Who Entertain

Being entertaining is a must for school and college speakers, because student audiences find it difficult to sit politely through a speech they consider boring!

It's no wonder that comedians and celebrities are popular on college campuses, while storytellers are popular in schools. However, virtually any topic can be made entertaining. Visit **http://homepage.mac.com/ stevenmichaelharris/schoolshow.htm** to see how Steven Michael Harris makes a "lecture on writing" into a crowd pleaser.

7.6.2   Potential Employers

Making It Count

Making It Count, a division of Monster.com, hires speakers to deliver programs to high schools and colleges. They hire part-time contract speakers to conduct programs on: Making College Count (for high school seniors), Making High School Count (for high school freshmen), Making Your College Search Count (juniors), and Unleash Your Inner Monster (college freshmen).

Recruiting for speakers is done in the spring and fall. They want to see a 5-10 minute video (it's okay to record yourself at home doing a dynamic speech to the camera), along with a resume and cover letter. Mail your materials to:

> Making It Count Programs
> Speaker Recruitment – MCSC/CC
> 10296 Springfield Pike
> Suite #500
> Cincinnati, OH 45215

You can find more information by visiting **www.speaker. makingitcount.com**.

Schools

To get booked to speak in a particular school, you can contact the school counselor, PTA (Parent-Teacher Association) or school principal. If you're phoning, it is usually easier to get through to the school counselor than the principal, so it's a good idea to approach the counselor first.

If you want to try sending out a mailing, you can get a list of members of the National Association of Secondary School Principals (NASSP). Visit **www.principals.org** (then click on "Marketing Opportunities" at the top of the page) or phone 703-860-0200 for information.

Curt Tueffert (**www.tueffert.com**), speaks to junior high, high school, and college students. He recommends for "a bigger bang for the buck" speakers should go to the school district and work with the decision-makers that can put together a program for multi-school functions.

Colleges

The decision-maker who hires speakers at most college campuses is the Student Activities Director, who typically works in a Student Activities

Office. See section 7.5.1 for information about contacting colleges (look for the "student activities" office instead of "continuing education").

A faster, easier way to get a list of decision-makers is to join the Association for the Promotion of Campus Activities (APCA). For a $199 annual membership fee, you will receive the *APCA Campus Market Directory*, a set of mailing labels and contact information for campus decision-makers across the country.

Your membership includes a one-year subscription to *Campus Activities Magazine*, with inside information on working in the campus marketplace. You will also be eligible to participate in speakers showcases at APCA conferences (read on to find out more about these showcases), and will have many networking opportunities with decision-makers.

Association for the Promotion of Campus Activities

Address: P.O. Box 4340
Sevierville, TN 37863

Phone: (800) 681-5031

Website: **www.apca.com**

7.6.3   Rates of Pay

Of course there are opportunities to speak for free both at schools and colleges. However, many speakers are paid to speak to these audiences.

Making College Count pays its contract speakers $100 to $250 per presentation. Josten's Speakers Bureau, which handles bookings for a number of speakers, will sometimes book a speaker into more than one school in an area. The speaker's fee for each booking on one of these "shared days" may be as low as $400. For a single booking in one day, the fee may range to as high as $2,500. (If you are booked through a speaker's bureau you will also pay the bureau a commission of about 25 percent of your earnings.)

According to speaker Andrea Kulberg (see her interview at the end of this section), the fee structure for school programs (Pre-K through 12th grade) tends to be slightly lower than collegiate or corporate events simply because of budget restrictions within public school systems.

Colleges have more resources for funding programs and they also expect to pay more for a quality speaker.

7.6.4 How to Improve Your Odds of Getting Hired

Help the School Find Funds for Your Talk

There are a number of ways to get funding for your presentation. If the school does not have the funds, it may be able to raise them from community groups or government agencies. Here are some ideas to help schools raise funds for your speeches:

- Check with the school's administration and see if funds are available from the Associated Student Body Fund.

- If your talk aims to prevent a problem such as drug use, drunk driving, violence, or teen pregnancy, grant money from the school district, county, state, or federal governments may be available. Contact your state or provincial department of education or human services to ask if they can refer you to appropriate programs.

- Check with the school's PTA to ask if they will contribute funds to support your program.

- Contact community organizations such as Rotary Club, Kiwanis, and Lions Club. These organizations provide financial support for a variety of community projects.

- You may be able to get support from local businesses by contacting the owner (if it's a small company) or the department responsible for donations (if it's a large company).

- See if another school in the area would have you speak on the same day. The two schools can split your speaker's fee.

Participate in Conferences

Colleges

One way to reach decision-makers in the college market is to participate in Speakers Showcases at national or regional conferences. During a showcase, speakers have the opportunity to present a brief (20-30 minute) program for an audience of decision-makers. A showcase is your opportunity to show decision-makers that you are the type of speaker they are looking for.

During your presentation you should use your best material, include personal stories that show you have "been there, done that," and entertain while you educate.

While you may only be "on stage" during the showcase, you can promote yourself throughout the conference by networking informally with decision-makers.

As mentioned, The Association for the Promotion of Campus Activities (ACPA) holds national conferences attended by hundreds of decision-makers, known as "campus talent buyers." Activities showcases featuring "artists" such as speakers are held throughout the conference. Immediately after these showcases, agencies, artists, and decision-makers meet in the exhibit hall to discuss business.

By joining ACPA, you can attend the conference (including sessions on marketing to college decision-makers), participate in the showcase, and get a booth at the exhibit hall – all for a single conference registration fee. Conferences are held in the spring and fall.

Conferences also provide an opportunity to participate in the APCA Cooperative Buying Program. This program allows schools attending the conference to merge their buying power by offering a block of speaking dates in exchange for a lower price and sharing of travel costs. For example, a speaker who charges $1,200 for a single speaking engagement might offer to speak for $1,100 per engagement for two dates within a three-day period. This is a win-win for the schools and the speaker.

If you are interested in speaking at Canadian colleges and universities, the organization to join in Canada is the Canadian Organization of Campus Activities. You can become an associate member for $275 per year (Canadian funds) and participate in showcases at their annual conferences.

You can contact them at:

Canadian Organization of Campus Activities

Address: 509 Commissioners Road W., Suite 202
               London, ON N6J 1Y5

Phone: (519) 690-0207

Website: **www.coca.org**

Schools

You can reach decision-makers by participating in annual conferences of the National Association of Secondary School Principals (NASSP) or the National Association for Student Activity Advisors, a group sponsored by the NASSP.

Although these assocations do not have speaker showcases at their conferences, speakers may promote themselves with an exhibit booth. For more information about how to reach these associations' members visit **www.principals.org** (then click on "Strategic Partners" under the "Information for" heading), or phone 703-860-0200.

Work With Speakers Bureaus

In chapter 8 you will learn about speakers bureaus, which are agencies that can help you get more bookings. Here are two in the school market:

Jostens Speakers Bureau

Address: P.O. Box 1488
               Lafayette, CA 94549

Phone: (800) 541-4660

Website: **www.jostensspeakersbureau.com**

Bureau of Lectures and Concert Artists

Address: 123 West 8th Street
               Suite 205
               Lawrence, KS 66044

Phone: (800) 255-0084

Website: **www.assemblyline.com**

Meet Successful School Speaker Andrea Kulberg

Andrea Kulberg attended the University of Texas in Austin where she obtained her Bachelor's Degree in Elementary Education. While in Austin, Andrea served as the country's first and only visually impaired collegiate cheerleader.

She was also a member of the National Cheerleaders Association (NCA) staff for three years, teaching cheerleaders of all ages at summer camps and choreographing for competitive squads. In August of 1997, Andrea completed her Master's Degree in Education at the University of Texas-Arlington with a 4.0 GPA as the Graduate Student of the Year.

Andrea enjoyed some wonderful experiences with students when she taught first grade in the Mansfield Independent School District near Dallas/Fort Worth. She has now taken the opportunity to have a bigger classroom of sorts as she dedicates her life to educating and inspiring people of all ages as a motivational and educational speaker.

Many parents, teens, and children have learned the "Skills of Success" through Andrea's motivational program, *From Try to Triumphant*, as she shares her unique perspective on overcoming adversity through her experiences as a disabled person, an educator, and an athlete. Andrea also travels to elementary schools to teach students about disabilities and other individual differences with her very popular program, *I Like To Be Me!* She also offers *The 20/20 Leadership Conference* for cheer coaches, captains and teams. You can read about Andrea's speaking programs at **www.futurecheer.net/about.htm**.

In December, 1999, Andrea and her husband, Neil, joyfully welcomed their beautiful baby girl, Caitlyn Renee Kulberg, into the world. They celebrated yet another miracle of life in February, 2000 when Andrea became a kidney cancer survivor. Neil, Andrea, and Caitlyn now look forward to spending many years together enjoying all the great things that life has to offer.

What age groups do you speak to?

I've spoken to groups of all ages – from preschool to retirement age – over the years. Some of these engagements were paid, but many were done for no fee.

When I decided to make my career as a professional speaker, however, I needed a starting place. I chose the elementary school market for several reasons. First of all, the elementary school market was the market I knew best and it was the market I had a passion for. My collegiate education was focused here and my prior work history was in the elementary schools. As a former teacher, I had a solid working knowledge of how the school systems and program funding worked. I also had an understanding of the demands made on teachers as they aimed to service 25 (or more) individual students – each with individual needs.

As a disabled person, I was able to identify with students who had obstacles to overcome in their learning processes, and these students in turn were able to identify with me. And most of all, I started my work in the elementary schools because I believe that the sooner we can get to kids, teach them to celebrate their differences, and believe in who they are, the better off they will be.

While I still plan on speaking in elementary schools, I will be expanding my scope to include more junior highs, high schools, colleges, and beyond in the future.

What topics do you speak on for schools?

My elementary program (*I Like To Be Me!*) is an educational storytelling program that focuses on teaching specifically about disabilities and visual impairments. I teach children how to correctly guide a blind person and show them some of the tools blind and visually impaired persons can use to make living in a sighted world more convenient.

That lesson is then expanded to discussions of all individual differences—from having freckles and red hair to different body shapes or skin color. Even children who do not speak English enjoy this very visual, humorous, high-energy program.

From Try to Triumphant is a motivational program I use to teach the specific skills needed to be successful. Generally done as a keynote, it is intended for Junior High and older groups including corporate and civic organizations. This program is always customized to meet the needs and individual circumstances of each audience.

What personal traits or speaking qualities do you think can help someone succeed as a school speaker?

As is the case with any speaker in any market, being able to take rejection and being able to persevere is the key to being successful. Most schools have many different program options to consider in allocating funds from their limited budgets. If a school opts to pass on your program, it is often not because they would not like to have you there, but because there are more options available to them than there is money.

Just remember that there are a lot of schools out there, so if you have a program of real value, persevere and sooner or later you will be hired to do your presentation. If you do a good job there, it will be easier to get more schools booked after that.

Another skill that will help you become successful as an educational speaker is professionalism. It sounds so logical, but it takes significant effort to carry yourself and manage your business this way. Professionalism from start to finish is always a priority. Remember that it will be impossible to sell the program if you don't first sell yourself, so no matter who you deal with along the way, treat them as a respected colleague and they will most likely (though not always) return the favor.

Speaking of treating others appropriately, don't forget about your audience. Students need to identify with the speaker quickly – say, in the first minute of the program. After that, they'll be looking for someone who respects their intelligence and is willing to work on their terms. Learning to be on the same level as the students is a fantastic way to grab your audience and help them retain what you are teaching.

If you're speaking to a group of first graders, for example, it's okay to get a little silly — they love it and will get silly right along with you! They'll have so much fun — you will have taught, inspired, and entertained them before they know what happened!

Who would a beginning speaker contact to get speaking engagements at schools?

One of the most difficult aspects of selling programs to schools is that each campus is run differently than the next, so there is no set way to approach the school and sell your program.

In general, I have found that school counselors and PTAs (Parent Teacher Associations) are usually a good place to start. The counselor is almost always in tune to what social skills the student body needs to learn about and the PTA is the organization that funds and plans school programs.

If the counselor and/or PTA are not able to find ways to fund your program but still wish to hire you, there may be discretionary funds still available within the school.

Oftentimes the principal is the person who oversees this kind of decision. I have found, however, that principals can be very difficult to reach via telephone, so if you choose to go that route, it would be best for you to make an appointment ahead of time and visit in person.

What would you recommend for a beginning speaker looking for mailing lists of contacts who hire school speakers?

I would suggest contacting your state's education agency for a list of the schools in your market. In my case, I contacted the Texas Education Agency and got a list of schools, addresses, and contacts online. I put the information into a database and used it to create mailing labels.

I sent out over 100 mailers to local schools on that list and started making some phone calls. I was initially disappointed in the lack of response I got – maybe two or three schools showed interest and only one followed through and actually hired me. But one school was enough because the program was successful and positive word of mouth can go a long way.

I still make calls and occasionally send out information in the mail, but much of what I do in the schools now is based on word of mouth – the greatest advertisement you can have.

What additional tips would you be willing to offer a beginning speaker who wanted to speak in schools?

If you want to be truly successful speaking in schools, don't do it for the money. Do it because you have a passion for the students and their well being. Believe in the kids you are talking to and they will learn to believe in themselves. That way, along with your paychecks, you'll get a lot of non-monetary rewards. There is nothing in the world better than knowing you just made a difference in someone's life. That is why I am so honored to be a professional speaker.

7.7 Cruise Ships

Speaking on a cruise ship is a wonderful way to combine business with pleasure. So how do you get one of these fabulous gigs?

At a seminar I was presenting for speakers, one of the participants had just returned from delivering a spouse program at a General Motors conference held on a cruise ship. Opportunities like that are sometimes a matter of luck – you get hired for an event that happens to be taking place on a cruise ship.

The techniques you would use to approach associations and other organizations are described in detail earlier in this chapter. In this section, you will find information about a more common cruise ship opportunity – getting hired by cruise lines.

7.7.1 Types of Opportunities

Cruise lines hire several different types of speakers:

- Experts in the culture, geography, history, or politics of a ship's destination.

- Instructors for activities such as arts and crafts, bridge, dancing and writing.

- Lecturers on topics that will interest a general audience (such as astrology, health, movies, the Internet, etc.).

- Youth Directors to present activities for young people.

As a lecturer, speaker or instructor, you will present two or more sessions per week when the ship is not in port. A session typically lasts from 45 to 60 minutes.

7.7.2   What it Pays

Cruise ships generally do not pay speakers. They provide a free cruise for you and a guest, and you are responsible for your own air fare and expenses, although air fare may be paid in some circumstances.

If you have been hired by a cruise line, they will likely not allow you to sell any products, although they may sell them through the gift shop. If you want to earn cash and sell your products, an alternative is to present your own seminars on a cruise ship. You choose an interesting topic to present, then promote the cruise as you would a seminar, with people "buying tickets" through the travel agent.

7.7.3   What These Employers Want

Above all, cruise ships want their guests to enjoy their cruise experience. To help them do so, they want to offer their guests a variety of interesting activities to choose from. In most cases they want their guests to have more than educational experiences – they want them to be entertained. Thus, although cruise ships hire "lecturers," they are actually seeking excellent speakers who can deliver with humor and plenty of audience involvement.

It is also important to note that cruise ships are generally looking for topics of personal interest, rather than business topics.

7.7.4   How to Improve Your Odds of Getting Hired

Contact the Right Department

While a "human resources" department may be the first contact, speakers are usually hired by the "entertainment" department. To find the department that can hire you when you phone a cruise line, explain that you are seeking a position in on-board entertainment.

Different cruise lines use different titles for these positions, including: lecturer, speaker, presenter, activity leader, instructor, or youth director. The programs may be referred to as "entertainment," "life enrichment," or "cultural enrichment."

Propose Popular Topics

Cruise ships want interesting programs that will be "crowd pleasers." When coming up with topics to propose, you may be able to get ideas from continuing education catalogs.

According to Julie Botteri, author of the *FabJob Guide to Get a Job on a Cruise Ship*, categories include "motivational, self improvement, health and nutrition, wine and food appreciation, creative writing, genealogy, and numerology." However, a number of cruise lines want "meatier" topics such as current events, politics, history, art, culture, and wildlife.

Submit Professional Materials

Like other employers, the people who hire cruise ship speakers want to see you in action. So submit a video showing your excellent presentation skills, along with your information package. When choosing the footage for your video, remember that the decision-maker will want to see that you use plenty of humor and audience participation.

Consider Using a Bureau

There are a number of bureaus, or agencies, that place speakers on cruise ships. Unlike a regular speakers bureau (described in chapter 8), these companies charge a fee to the speaker. A typical fee is $25-$50 per day of the cruise. Some bureaus are listed in the next section.

7.7.5   Potential Employers

Cruise Lines

A number of cruise lines offer employment information by telephone or at their websites. If you want to contact cruise lines directly you will find information about several cruise lines below. Links to other cruise lines can be found at **www. raynorshyn.com/cruises**.

Carnival Cruise Lines

Carnival Cruise Lines is the world's most popular cruise line. Although their website (**www.carnival.com**) does not have information about applying to be a lecturer, you can find out how to apply by calling (305) 599-2600. When the recorded message comes on, press "2" for the employment line, then press "9" for the entertainment department.

Crystal Cruises

Crystal Cruises hires "Destination Lecturers" and "Special Interest Lecturers." Phone their corporate offices at (310) 785-9300 and ask to be put through to the entertainment department or check opportunities on their website at **www.crystalcruises.com/employment.aspx**. (Click on "Shipboard Positions - Entertainment.")

Holland America

Holland America hires speakers with expertise in the history, culture, geography, anthropology, or politics of the places they visit. For information about how to apply, visit **www.hollandamericaentertainment. com/enrichment.asp**.

Princess Cruises

Princess Cruises has a shipboard employment hotline at (800) 872-6779, and an employment information page at their website, located at **http:// employment.princess.com** (click on "Shipboard" under "Employment").

Norwegian Cruise Lines

The Norwegian Cruise Lines website has shipboard employment opportunities. Visit **http://164.109.173.40/employment/ncl/index.htm** and click on "View Job Opportunities." Look under "Entertainment" for openings.

Bureaus for Cruise Ship Speakers

Many cruise lines, including Celebrity Cruises, Princess Cruises, Royal Caribbean and Radisson Seven Seas Cruises, use bureaus to find speakers. The following have opportunities for speakers on cruise ships:

Bramson Entertainment Bureau

Address: 630 Ninth Avenue, Suite 203
New York, NY 10036

Phone: (212) 265-3500

Website: **www.bramson.com**

Compass Speakers and Entertainment, Inc.

Address: 2455 East Sunrise Blvd, Suite 804
Ft. Lauderdale, FL 33304

Phone: (954) 568-3801

Website: **http://compassspeakers.com**

Sixth Star Entertainment and Marketing

Address: 21 NW 5th Street
Fort Lauderdale, FL 33301

Phone: (954) 462-6760

Website: **www.sixthstar.com**

8. Speakers Bureaus

8.1 How a Bureau Works

A speakers bureau acts as a liaison between speakers and employers, by finding speakers to present speeches for a variety of clients. Here are some typical steps in the process:

1. A client, such as an association meeting planner, calls a speakers bureau and explains that they need a keynote speaker for an upcoming conference. The meeting planner and bureau representative discuss the association's needs, the conference topic and speaker budget.

2. The bureau representative goes through the bureau's database of speakers and finds several speakers who seem like they fit well with the association's needs.

3. The bureau contacts the speakers to see if they are available to speak on the conference date. If so, the speakers are asked to put a "hold" on the date. (A hold is like a tentative booking. It means the date is unavailable for other speaking engagements.)

4. The bureau sends speakers' information packages and demo videos to the meeting planner.

5. The meeting planner reviews the speaker information and, working alone or in consultation with others, chooses a speaker to deliver the keynote speech.

6. The meeting planner informs the bureau of their choice.

7. The bureau informs the chosen speaker (and those who were not chosen), sends contracts to both the meeting planner and the speaker, and arranges for the speaker to be paid by the association. In return for the booking, the bureau receives a commission of 25 to 35 percent from the speaker's fee.

This is how it works in theory. In practice, getting bookings through a speakers bureau is not always this easy. There are a number of factors that can get in the way of a bureau booking you.

Getting the Client to Call in the First Place

Bureaus find speakers at no cost to the client. (They are paid from speaker commissions.) So you might think that bureaus have plenty of work. Some do. But for many bureaus, getting clients is an ongoing struggle that requires constant marketing effort. Many bureaus, especially those just starting out, are swamped with calls from speakers seeking work, but receive relatively few calls from clients seeking speakers.

Getting the Bureau to Choose You

Once a bureau does get a call from the client, you want them to put your name forward for any speeches that you could do. This involves two steps: (1) getting into the bureau's database, and (2) becoming one of the bureau's "preferred" speakers. Both of these are covered in section 8.2.

Clients May Contact Several Bureaus

A bureau may invest time and resources finding excellent speakers for a client to choose from — only to have the client choose a speaker from a competing bureau. There is nothing to prevent a client from having a number of bureaus all working to find a speaker for the same event.

The Client's Plans May Change

A client may choose a speaker from a bureau, then change their mind before a contract is signed. For example, they may decide that the keynote speaker should be an industry expert rather than a motivational speaker. A meeting planner may quit, and the new one decides to use a different speaker. Budget cutbacks may mean a regional conference is cancelled.

There are any number of things that can happen, so smart bureau reps, like smart speakers, know that nothing is firm until it is in writing.

8.2 Getting a Bureau to Choose You

As mentioned above, there are two steps to being "chosen" by a speakers bureau.

8.2.1 Getting Into a Bureau's Database

The first step is for the bureau to accept you as one of their speakers.

What Bureaus Want

Virtually all bureaus want to represent celebrity speakers, so if you are a local or national celebrity you will be welcomed by most bureaus.

Most bureaus also represent experienced professional speakers. Although there are a few bureaus that accept speakers with low fees, some will only accept speakers earning at least $3,000 per keynote. They may also expect you to have references from paid speaking engagements. One bureau says they expect a speaker to have 20 such references!

> TIP: Before sending your materials to a bureau, call to find out what they want. Don't waste your time sending materials to bureaus that clearly are not a "fit" for you.

Finding Bureau Contact Information

The first place to look for speakers bureaus is in your own community. Try checking the Yellow Pages under "Speakers Services" or "Public Speaking." Online, you can try a search engine using the keywords "speakers bureaus." You can also find bureaus listed by country, state, and city at **www.findspeakersandbureaus.com**. You will need to register (it's free) to access the information at this site.

The *International Directory of Agencies and Bureaus* lists hundreds of agents and bureaus around the world. You can receive a copy of the directory by purchasing a subscription to *Sharing Ideas* magazine for $100 ($124 in Canada). You can find out more information at **www.speakandgrowrich. com/sharing_ideas_overview.htm**.

Send Them Your Materials

Most bureaus want an information package and video from speakers. To find out exactly what a bureau wants from you, you can call them or check their website. Following are examples of the types of materials that bureaus want:

- Professional video demo

- Biography and one-sheet

- Photos of you

- Fee schedule

- References from clients

- Samples of books or articles

> TIP: It would cost thousands of dollars to send your information package and demo video to every bureau in the country, so be selective about which bureaus to approach. Instead of trying to get listed with hundreds of bureaus, focus instead on becoming a "preferred" speaker with a few bureaus.

8.2.2   Becoming a "Preferred" Speaker

To get booked through a speakers bureau you need to do more than simply get into their database of speakers. Many bureaus have thousands – or tens of thousands – of speakers in their database. When a client calls for a motivational speaker, the bureau may have hundreds of speakers who could do the job.

The speakers who will actually be recommended to the client are the bureau's preferred speakers. A preferred speaker is any speaker who:

- Has developed a relationship with bureau representatives

- Is easy to work with

- Can be depended upon to do an excellent job

- Will make the bureau look good to the client

For these reasons, preferred speakers are the first ones bureaus call when a job is available. Bureaus do not have a formal set of criteria that determines who will become a preferred speaker. In other words, if you phone up a bureau and say, "I would like to become one of your preferred speakers," you will have to explain what you are talking about.

Instead, you can become a preferred speaker informally, by following some of the suggestions that follow.

Select Some Bureaus You Would Like to Work With

When you call bureaus to find out what they want, you may be able to get a sense of what they would be like to work with.

Some questions to ask yourself:

- Is the telephone answered professionally?

- Are you put through to someone who actually works with speakers?

- Does the bureau represent speakers in your fee range?

- Are you treated with respect?

Invite Them to See You Speak

Before recommending a speaker, bureaus usually like to see that speaker in action. So invite representatives of local bureaus to see you speak. Section 6.3 offers ideas for inviting people to your speeches.

Let Them Know You Will Go the Extra Mile

Because bureaus are often in competition with each other, they are grateful for speakers who can help them land the job.

Here are a couple of ways you can help your bureau:

- Prepare a customized one-sheet tailored to the specific needs of the client. For example, you could revise the title of your speech to correspond with the topic of the client's conference.

- Talk about the program with the client to answer questions, explain how your speech will meet their needs, and help sell them on hiring you.

Of course if you are willing to help out in these ways be sure to let the bureau know.

Pass on Leads

When you get a booking through a bureau, any spin-off business from the client or anyone else who hears that speech should go through the bureau. This isn't just a nice thing to do – bureaus expect it.

To really make an impression on a bureau, pass on brand new leads. For example, if someone contacts you for a speech and you are already booked, it's not a topic you speak on, it doesn't pay what you want, or you're simply not interested, why not pass it on to a bureau?

Don't simply suggest the client call the bureau. Instead, take the information and call the bureau yourself. Speak with the bureau representative you are developing a relationship with, and give them the lead. Then call back the client and give them the information about the bureau.

Keep in Touch

Keeping in touch does not mean adding a bureau to a mailing list to receive frequent promotional mailings. Many bureaus are swamped with speaker materials and are turned off by mass mailings that don't offer new information. If you do send out a newsletter, make sure it offers information of value to the bureau owner.

A better way to stay in touch is to develop genuine business relationships with a few bureau owners or representatives. This might involve:

- Meeting for coffee

- Treating them to lunch

- Calling a couple of times a month (more or less, depending on your relationship) to catch up and share industry news

- Sending thank-you gifts after a speech they have booked for you

- Inviting them as your guest to a networking event

- Passing on information of interest to them

- Sending a gift for the holiday season

- Inviting them to social events at your home

Participate in Showcases

A speakers showcase is an event, usually sponsored by a speakers bureau, that provides an opportunity for prospective employers to see live presentations by a variety of speakers. Each speaker delivers a presentation of 20 minutes or so, and has an opportunity to mingle with decision-makers during breaks. Any bookings that result from the showcase are done through the bureau that sponsors it.

If you are invited to participate in a showcase by a bureau you want to work closely with, you should consider doing it. Be aware, however, that you will probably be expected to pay a fee of several hundred dollars to participate to help cover the bureau's expenses in putting on the event.

As there is no guarantee you will be booked as a result of a showcase, it is recommended that you participate only if you see other benefits, such as strengthening your relationship with your bureau or getting footage for your video.

8.3   A Few Cautions About Bureaus

While most bureaus are run by professionals, a few are not. Anyone can set up a business in their basement and call it a "speakers bureau." To protect yourself, a little healthy caution is in order.

> **IMPORTANT NOTE:**
> Bureaus that have been mentioned in this book are included for the convenience of readers only. They are not recommendations. Only you can determine which bureaus will be best for you.

Be Cautious of "Exclusive" Contracts

An exclusive contract with a bureau prevents you from getting bookings through any other bureau. It simply isn't necessary to agree to such a condition. Furthermore, you risk losing business. I know an outstanding speaker who made the mistake of signing an exclusive contract with a bureau which did not get him a single booking. Fortunately, after a year he was able to get out of the contract.

Be Cautious of Bureaus That Charge Fees

Some bureaus charge "registration fees" of hundreds of dollars. Others charge annual or monthly fees.

Successful bureaus make their money from speaker commissions. If a bureau is charging fees, you should investigate them to ensure that speaker fees are not their primary source of revenue. Ask for references from speakers they represent, and check with speakers they represent who they haven't given as references to find out how much work the speakers are getting through the bureau.

Realize that even if other speakers are getting bookings, there is a risk the bureau may not get bookings for you. Sign up only if you can afford to lose the fee.

Be Cautious of Bureaus Selling Other Services

Some companies that call themselves "speakers bureaus" are actually in the business of selling services to speakers (such as speaking seminars, marketing services, publishing consulting, and speech coaching). All of these services can be wonderful, and my concern is not with bureaus that offer them in addition to getting bookings for clients. The problem arises if a company that calls itself a bureau does not actually get bookings for speakers.

EXAMPLE:

I knew of a company that placed Yellow Pages ads claiming to be a bureau. In fact, they only booked speeches for the company's owners. When they were contacted by speakers looking for work, they would aggressively sell a speaking seminar by suggesting that it could lead to work through the bureau.

If you buy such a service, do so because you want the service, not because you hope it will lead to work through the bureau.

Be Cautious of Bureaus Run by Speakers

Some speakers set up a bureau to market themselves along with other speakers. If you speak on the same topic as a bureau owner, you may find yourself competing for business with the person who is representing you.

Which reminds me of a story...

A bureau owner called to ask if I would be willing to give a 20-minute keynote to a non-profit group for a $200 fee. It was far below my usual fee, but he assured me it could result in spin-off business. I agreed to give the talk and worked hard to customize and deliver an excellent speech.

Immediately after the speech I was approached by an audience member. "I would like to hire you to speak to our department," she said. Of course I was delighted.

"You'll have to speak to my speaker's bureau," I replied, and went to find the bureau owner who had attended the event. I introduced him to the client, and she explained that she wanted to hire me. I will never forget what he said next:

"Oh, we have plenty of speakers who could do that. Why don't I give you a call and we can discuss who would be best for your group."

The woman looked surprised. "Why would I want anyone else when I can have Tag?" she very kindly said in my defence.

"Because we have lots of other speakers," he answered. "Someone else may be better for your group. I'll call you next week to discuss it."

I was so shocked I was speechless. Later that day I phoned and told him that what he had done was every speaker's greatest fear. He apologized and said it was because he was still new to the speaking business, and was simply excited about the possible booking. He promised that if he landed the contract, I would get the job.

I did not get the job, and unfortunately did not have the woman's name or department so I could not follow up myself.

I later learned that the bureau owner had decided to launch a speaking career of his own. While there may have been other reasons I didn't get the contract, it is not wise to be competing against the person who is representing you to potential clients!

TIP: With spin-off business, contact the bureau only when you are ready to send out a contract to the client.

9. Being Successful on the Job

This guide has already given you many ideas to help you launch your career as a motivational speaker. In this section you will find some additional insights and advice. The information that follows can help you:

- Get more work

- Earn more money

- Achieve even greater success as a motivational speaker

9.1 Ask "What Else Can I Do?"

Whenever you are hired to speak, find out if there are opportunities for additional work. Say to the employer, "Since I will be there anyway, let's see if there are any other ways I can be of service."

For example, if you are booked to present a keynote speech or to lead a session at a conference you could also offer to:

- Present a spouse program

- Speak at a meal

- Emcee an introductory get-together on the first night of the conference

- Present additional breakout sessions

Or you could offer to come a day early to do any of the following:

- Present a "pre-conference" workshop on a related topic

- Offer individual or small group consulting to key people in the organization

- Carry out media publicity

Organizations are often happy to have speakers do additional work because they save on the travel costs of hiring another speaker. In some cases you may be able to get your full fee for the extra work you do.

> **EXAMPLE:**
> When Clayton and I were invited to present a two hour session on "What does the opposite sex want?" at a singles conference in Vancouver, we told the organizer we could also speak on a number of other topics. She booked us to present a session on "How to meet people" immediately after our first session. We doubled our earnings for the day simply by asking.

If it will help to make the sale, you might offer to present additional sessions at a reduced price. For example, you could offer to do a second session for a 25 or 50 percent discount because you probably would not be able to get a second booking for that day anyway.

9.2 Sell Products

One way to increase your income is by selling products at your speeches. This is often referred to as "back of the room" or BOR sales, because the table where a speaker's products are for sale has traditionally been located at the back of the room.

Some speakers earn so much from product sales that they are willing to speak for free to have an audience to sell to. Depending on a variety of factors (such as the size of the audience), product sales may result in thousands of dollars in additional income per speech. Here are some tips on how to sell products:

- Refer to your products during your talk, but don't overdo it. Your audience will respond negatively if they feel that you're selling to them during your speech. One way to subtly mention a product during your speech is to ask for a volunteer from the audience to assist you with something, then reward them with the product.

- Donate part of your profits to charity. Find out what charities the organization supports and announce you'll donate a percentage of sales to those charities.

- Put a product order form at the bottom or on the back of your speaker evaluation sheets.

- Bundle a set of materials together (for instance, a book, a video and a CD) and sell the set at a discount.

- Accept credit cards as a form of payment. Contact your financial instuitution to apply to become a credit card merchant.

You can consider selling things like books, reports, CDs, software, calendars, T-shirts, bookmarks, posters, coffee mugs, bumper stickers, caps, greeting cards, or anything else you can think of. You can create promotional products to resell through a site such as **www.cafepress.com**.

9.2.1   Producing Your Own Products

If you want to publish a book or other items mentioned above, you can get price quotes from printers at **www.printindustry.com**.

If you only have enough material for an article or booklet, you can desktop publish that onto 8 1/2" x 11" sheets, staple the sheets together, and sell it as a "special report."

The amount you can charge for a book or report depends on how valuable people consider your information to be. I suggest experimenting with different prices at different speeches. For example, my partner Clayton and I self-published a book that cost about $2.00 to print. We experimented with a variety of sale prices ($9.95 at one speech, $19.95 at another speech, etc.) and found that the price at which it consistently sold the most copies the most profitably was $14.95.

You can find additional helpful information about self-publishing by reading some books on the subject. I recommend *The Complete Guide to Self-Publishing*, by Tom and Marilyn Ross, and *The Self-Publishing Manual*, by Dan Poynter.

As a beginning speaker, the quickest way to develop audio and video material is by recording a live presentation, using the methods described in section 6.4. You can find companies that duplicate audio and video materials in the Yellow Pages, or by doing an online search for "duplication services." An example of such a company is CDI Media, located at **www.cdimedia.com** or CD/DVD Now at **www.cddvdnow.com**. You can get other products through a site such as CafePress.com at **www. cafepress.com**.

9.2.2   Selling Other People's Products

An excellent way to have products to sell at your speeches is to sell other people's products. For example, if you were giving a speech on success, you could find books, tapes or other products related to success, and sell them to people attending your speech.

Virtually any publisher will sell you "bulk" copies (i.e. more than a few copies) at a price discount. The discount will vary depending on the product and how many copies you want.

However, most book publishers offer bookstores a 40 percent discount if they buy as few as five books, with higher discounts for larger quantities. With a 40 percent discount, you would be paying only $6.00 for a book that retails for $10.00. When you resold the book at your speech, you would pocket the profit of $4.00.

9.3   Connect With Other Speakers

By connecting with other speakers you may be able to learn about speaking opportunities as well as benefit from the experiences of those who are already successful in the business. Following are the best ways to connect with other speakers:

9.3.1 Subscribe to SpeakerNet News

SpeakerNet News is a free weekly e-mail newsletter which is sent out each Friday. Edited by professional speakers Rebecca Morgan and Ken Braly, it offers a wealth of information and advice from professional speakers on topics such as marketing yourself, presentation skills, running your business, travel, technology, and other topics related to being a successful speaker.

SpeakerNet News also offers teleseminars on topics of interest to speakers such as "How to Get Speakers Bureaus to Call YOU" and "Creating Visual Aids that 'Wow' Your Audience." The cost is $25 per teleseminar. Visit **www.speakernetnews.com/tsem** for more information.

9.3.2 Speakers Organizations

Speakers organizations provide a variety of opportunities for you to connect with and learn from professional speakers. Contact the chapter nearest you for further information.

National Speakers Association

Since 1973 the National Speakers Association (NSA) has been providing services and educational programs to improve the business skills and platform performance of professional speakers in the United States. Among the services the NSA offers are:

- Conventions and workshops

- *Professional Speaker Magazine*

- The Certified Speaking Professional (CSP) designation

- *Who's Who in Professional Speaking* directory

To be eligible for professional membership in NSA, you must have made 20 fee-paid speeches or earned $25,000 in speaking fees in the past 12 months. Membership costs $425 per year, plus a fee of $175 for initial registration.

As a beginner, you may be able to attend career seminars or participate in an apprentice program which gives you the opportunity to learn from an experienced member. You can find local programs by contacting your local NSA chapter. For more information and to see a list of chapters, visit **www.nsaspeaker.org** or call (480) 968-2552.

Canadian Association of Professional Speakers

CAPS members have access to the NSA's programs and services and can also participate in local and national events.

Membership in CAPS costs $425, plus a $150 initiation fee. You can become a Candidate Member if you have earned income from 10 fee-paid speaking engagements at any time in your life. To become an Associate Member, you must have made 10 fee-paid speeches in the last 12 months. To become a Professional Member you must have made 20 fee-paid speeches or earned $25,000 in speaking fees in the past 12 months.

You can find information about CAPS and its local chapters at **www. canadianspeakers.org** or by calling (416) 847-3355.

Other Organizations

National Speakers Association of Australia

Website: **www.nationalspeakers.asn.au**

Phone: 1800 090 024

National Speakers Association of New Zealand

Website: **www.nationalspeakers.org.nz**

Phone: 64 9 622 0268

Professional Speakers Association (Europe)

Website: **www.professionalspeakers.org**

Phone: 44 (0) 845 3700 504

9.3.3   Develop Relationships

An excellent way to connect with professional speakers is to attend the speeches, seminars, and workshops they present. Of course this is a great learning opportunity, but beyond listening to them speak, take the opportunity to introduce yourself on a break, ask for their business card, and let them know you will be calling to invite them for coffee.

By establishing a relationship with a professional speaker, you may not only learn more about the speaking business, you may actually get some work as a result.

EXAMPLE:
A woman named Leeanne who attended one of my seminars made an impression on me by treating me to lunch and volunteering to help out at my future seminars. She also offered me a free table to promote my book at a conference she was involved with.

I remembered Leeanne when I was asked to speak on time management at a conference of herbalists. It paid only a few hundred dollars and wasn't my specialty, so I called to ask if she would be interested in the job. She jumped at the opportunity, then followed up with an enthusiastic thank-you e-mail.

A few months later I needed another speaker to fill in for me at the annual meeting of a chapter of the International Association of Administrative Professionals. Who do you think I called? That's right, Leeanne.

To establish a relationship with a professional speaker, offer them something of value. A free lunch is a start, but it's better to volunteer your services or share information. And always remember to thank them for any work they send your way!

You could also propose an unpaid internship, where you would help out in the speaker's office on a part-time basis at no charge to the speaker. This can be a win-win for both of you. The speaker benefits from your help while you learn from the speaker.

9.3.4 Speaking Coaches

If you want a more formal arrangement, consider hiring a professional speaker to coach you. Coaches may provide services such as coaching on presentation skills, image consulting, or marketing advice. They may provide coaching by e-mail, phone, or in person.

Prices vary widely, and may range from $50 per hour to thousands of dollars. Many coaches also offer books, tapes, newsletters, and seminars as well as free articles on their websites.

We cannot say which coach, if any, will be best for you. You are the only one who can make that decision. Before hiring a coach, you should do your homework to learn more about the coach and clarify exactly what services they will provide and for what cost.

You may be able to find coaches by networking with other speakers or doing an online search for the term "speaking coaching." Following are some of the professional speakers who provide services for speakers. Visit their websites for further information and articles.

- *Jane Atkinson*
  www.speakerlauncher.com

- *Lois Creamer*
  www.bookmorebusiness.com

- *Paul Evans*
  www.instantspeakingsuccess.com/spk.htm

- *Patricia Fripp, CSP*
  www.fripp.com

- *Lenny Laskowski*
  www.ljlseminars.com

- *Vickie Sullivan*
  www.sullivanspeaker.com

- *Alan Weiss*
  www.summitconsulting.com/mentor.html

9.4 Go the Extra Mile

Although many organizations like to bring in new keynote speakers every year, you can lay the groundwork to be invited back in the future, and help create positive word of mouth by going the extra mile for everyone who hires you.

Going the extra mile means more than being cooperative and pleasant to everyone you meet. It also means more than customizing your speech (employers expect your speech to be customized to their group). It means doing things to make the event organizer's job easier and making it more memorable for participants. Here are some ideas of things you can do to make a great impression.

- Write articles for their newsletter.

- Conduct telephone interviews with the media.

- Acknowledge and thank the organizer during your presentation.

- Attend the social event before the conference to meet participants.

- Arrive early to your talk and mingle with audience members.

- Give small gifts to all participants, such as:

    - An inspirational poem suitable for framing.

    - A list of dos and don'ts.

    - A list of the top 10 tips on your topic.

    - A certificate.

    - The gift item you include in your information package.

- Give an enthusiastic speech – no matter how tired you are.

- Of course you will stick around afterward to speak with audience members.

- Send a thank you letter to the organizer after the event.

9.5 Present Your Own Seminars

When you present your own seminar you pay the bills and handle the administrative details, but you can also reap large rewards. The benefits of presenting your own seminars include:

- You can invite prospective employers to see you speak.

- People who pay to attend the seminar may turn out to be employers, or they may recommend you to employers.

- Once you have presented a seminar on a particular topic you can tell prospective employers that you have spoken on that topic.

- Seminars can be an excellent source of testimonials to help you get future work.

- Your seminars can provide content for your demo materials.

- Seminars provide good practice to improve your speaking skills.

- The seminar itself may be a source of income. Some seminar presenters earn thousands of dollars per seminar.

Whether your purpose is to get speaking experience, to market yourself or to make money, there are a number of tasks that must be handled to ensure your seminar is a success, including the following. (A checklist of other major tasks is included in the CD-ROM.)

- Choose a topic and title

- Decide who your audience is

- Choose a date and time

- Book the location

- Set the registration fee

- Market the seminar

- Register people

- Prepare for the seminar

Many of the tips given elsewhere in this book can be used in presenting seminars. For example, section 2.1 explains how to choose a topic, and the advice and resources given in section 7.4.2 for developing training programs can also be used to develop seminars. This part of the guide therefore provides additional tips specifically for presenting your own seminars.

9.5.1   Deciding Who Your Audience Is

As mentioned in section 2.6, you can define your audience by a variety of characteristics. If you offer a seminar that doesn't attract a lot of people, you may need to change the title or fee (see below). However, you may also want to consider aiming it at a different audience.

EXAMPLE:
Several years ago I developed a seminar for small business owners on "How to Get Publicity for Your Business." It explained how to attract customers while saving thousands of dollars on advertising. Despite being an official event of the Chamber of Commerce, with a registration fee of just $49, only five business owners registered. Too late, I realized I was asking busy people to give up a full day for something that was a relatively low priority compared to their other concerns (such

as handling customers, collecting money, etc.). So I made some minor adjustments to the seminar, changed the title, and aimed it at a new audience – medium to large corporations and non-profit organizations. They did not need to be convinced of the value of publicity. The result is that I successfully sold the same seminar to many more people – for up to $179 per registration.

Small business owners are tough to reach because they find it so hard to take time away from their businesses. In fact, any audience that consists of people with a scarcity of time or money are not good prospects. For example, unless you are offering a free or very inexpensive seminar, it is not wise to present financial seminars for people with money issues. The people who need your seminar will not attend!

> **TIP:**   Some seminar companies have tremendous success with expensive financial seminars. They do it by offering people a free (i.e. no-risk) introductory seminar as part of a "two-step" program. (The second step is an expensive financial seminar.) Only a tiny percentage of the people who attend the introductory seminar register for the more expensive seminar, but that percentage is enough to keep those seminar companies experiencing plenty of "prosperity."

9.5.2   Choosing the Best Date and Time

At one of my seminars for speakers I was approached by a man who was having difficulty getting people to register for his seminars. He was receiving lots of inquiries, but wasn't able to actually get them to register. The problem? He was offering a seminar on how to overcome procrastination, advertising "classes start every four weeks."

While most of us wouldn't make this mistake, some seminar presenters will advertise "call for upcoming dates." Their thinking is: when enough people call, a seminar will be scheduled. However, when no date is advertised, many people ignore it. It's not urgent. The brochure gets filed away in that pile of documents we plan to look at "when there's more time." So set a date for your seminar. This will give potential registrants a deadline and encourage them to take action.

Don't worry too much about choosing the wrong date. Low turn-outs are often blamed on the "wrong date," but I believe few seminars fail for this reason alone. You can hold a seminar at almost any time of year and, regardless of what else is going on at the same time, have an excellent turn-out if you are offering something people are genuinely interested in. Likewise, if people are not interested in the topic, it does not matter how convenient your date and time are.

Best Months for Seminars

Although you can hold seminars at almost any time of the year, some dates are better than others. It seems that people of all ages are ready to "go back to school" in September and January. For many seminar presenters, September is the best month for registrations, while January is next best. While the number of registrations will depend on many factors besides the date, we have found that if we get 50 registrations for a seminar in April or November, we may get 150 in September and 100 in late January.

You should avoid late December because people are busy with the holiday season. To maximize registrations also stay away from any statutory holidays or long weekends, and avoid competing with popular local events.

Best Days of the Week

The day of the week is also an important factor in getting registrations. If organizations will be paying to send their employees to the seminar, the seminar can be held any weekday during business hours (Tuesday, Wednesday, and Thursday are best). If participants are paying their own way, you'll have the best turnout if you schedule the seminar for a Saturday or an evening.

Best Times of Day

For participants who are attending on their own time, an evening seminar is usually easier to fit into their schedule than a Saturday seminar. The difference in registrations can be dramatic. It is not unusual to get twice as many registrants for an evening seminar as for a full day seminar. An evening seminar can be scheduled to start at 6:00, 6:30 or 7:00 p.m., and should ideally end no later than 10:00 p.m. with one or two coffee breaks.

However, if you are expecting most registrants to be sent by their employers, make sure you do not schedule a seminar during an evening. People do not want to "work" during their time off. (Yes, the same seminar someone would gladly attend in their spare time if they are paying their own registration fee is considered "work" if their employer is paying!) A half day seminar should therefore be scheduled for a weekday morning or afternoon.

Daytime seminars should ideally start no earlier than 8:00 a.m. on a weekday or 9:00 a.m. on a Saturday, with registration starting a half hour or an hour before that (depending on the number of participants). Consider taking your lunch break at 11:45 a.m. so participants can beat the rush at local restaurants, and allow for at least one coffee break in both the morning and afternoon.

If you want your audience to stay with you, mentally as well as physically, make sure you finish no later than 5:00 p.m. It's even better if you can finish by 4:00 p.m. No matter how interested participants are, it can be difficult to remain attentive through a program of much more than six hours (seven hours, including lunch).

9.5.3   Booking the Location

If you have meeting rooms at your office, you can hold a seminar there. You may also be able to rent an inexpensive meeting room at a public library, educational institution, or business center.

However, if convenience and image are important to you, I suggest holding your seminar at a hotel or convention center. Using a good hotel or convention center can give your seminar credibility among potential registrants. These facilities also have employees who can advise you on room layouts, handle room set-up, and book audio-visual equipment.

If you want to use a hotel in another city, you'll need to do some detective work. A name brand hotel in your city may be luxurious and well-respected, but in another city it may be located in a run-down part of town. Check out facilities online, and consider contacting the local Chamber of Commerce or Convention and Visitors Bureau. While they are unlikely to tell you which hotel is "best," you could ask for "a list of luxury hotels that are centrally located."

What to Discuss with the Catering Coordinator

If you are booking a meeting room at a hotel or convention center, you will need to speak with someone in the sales or catering office. (If you're booking a room at a facility such as a library, ask the receptionist to put you through to the person responsible for renting meeting rooms.) The catering coordinator will ask you the date of your seminar, how many people you expect, and what room layout you want.

A room laid out in "theater style" (chairs only) will allow you to fit at least twice as many people into a room as "classroom style" (tables and chairs), but if your participants will do a lot of writing or if you expect a small group, arrange for tables. If you don't know how many people to expect, or if there's a possibility the seminar may be cancelled, try to book the facility on a tentative basis until you are sure it will go ahead.

> TIP: You may be able to reduce the rental cost for your meeting room simply by asking. If the price is high, tell them you are on a budget and ask if they can do any better on the price. If the facility is not booked, they may be willing to make a deal. We have had the price reduced by up to 50 percent this way.

Another money saving tip is not to provide a meal. Many seminar companies have found that meals are the number one source of complaints, and people who don't like the meal may feel negatively about the entire seminar! Perhaps an even more important reason not to serve a meal is that it may have virtually no impact on registrations. You may hear the odd grumble from someone who was hoping for a free lunch, but it very likely will not affect their decision to register, and the grumbles will likely be a lot fewer than if you do serve a meal.

However, your participants will appreciate refreshments such as coffee, tea, bottled water, and juice. It's nice to serve muffins and fruit in the morning, and cookies for an afternoon snack – but it's not required. The CD-ROM provided with this guide includes a helpful checklist of other items you may want to discuss with the catering coordinator.

9.5.4 Setting the Registration Fee

If your goal is to make money, some things to consider when setting your fee are who your audience is, whether you are offering valuable information that isn't available from other sources, and how confident you are in your ability to convince people of the seminar's value. If other organizations offer similar programs, you can check out their fees by reviewing catalogs from seminar companies and continuing education programs such as those listed in sections 7.3 and 7.5.

Prices for business seminars vary widely (for interpersonal communications seminars, I found fees ranging from $59 to over $800 per day). Your seminar will be easier to sell to companies if you come in on the low end (e.g. $149). For seminars offered to the general public, we found a fee of $49 was most popular.

You may be able to charge more for your seminar without reducing the number of registrations if:

- You are offering highly specialized or technical information

- You are affiliated with a respected institution such as a university

- Your seminar has just been featured in a newspaper story

- Your seminar has high perceived value

Free and Low Cost Seminars

If you are not concerned about making a profit from the seminar, you may want to consider charging only a nominal registration fee or even offering it free to all or some of the participants. Assuming the topic is an interesting one, this tactic may help to draw a crowd. Having a large audience can be helpful for video clips and can make a good impression on decision-makers who attend as guests.

Of course, there's really no such thing as a "free" seminar to participants. Attending a seminar still involves an investment of time, so you will need to convince people to register. We found it takes as much effort to convince someone to spend $12 to attend a singles evening with a speaker and wine and cheese reception, as it takes to convince somone to spend $49 to attend an evening singles seminar without any food or drink! In fact, a price that seems "too good to be true" can raise suspicion in the mind of people who are attending, who may wonder "what else will they try to sell me?"

TIP: One way to increase registrations is by offering a "bring a friend" discount. For example, the fee might be $49, or $39 each for two or more who register together.

9.5.5   Marketing the Seminar

The best way to market an upcoming seminar – with the greatest number of registrations for the lowest cost – is to get a feature story about the seminar published in a local newspaper. Section 6.5.2 has excellent advice to help you get media publicity. However, as it's unlikely you will get a major news story written before every seminar, you will need to use other marketing techniques. Following are some techniques that may be effective, depending on whether you are marketing your seminar to businesses or the public.

Direct Mail

Most business seminars are marketed through direct mail (mailing brochures to people who might be interested in attending). If you decide to use direct mail you can create your own mailing list or rent one.

One way to create your own list is to use a directory. For example, if you are a member of an organization such as the Chamber of Commerce, you might be able to find contact information for thousands of businesses in the organization's membership directory. Of course another excellent way to get names and addresses for your list is by distributing evaluation forms at your speeches.

To rent a list, you could contact an association or magazine publisher to see if they are willing to let you use their list. Online, search for "mailing lists" or "mailing list broker" (a broker can give you advice about the best lists to choose) or check the Yellow Pages under "mailing lists." Brokers and companies that sell lists can help you find lists broken down by geographic area, number of employees, industry, etc.

Buying a list from a broker or list company typically costs about 5 to 25 cents per name. With the cost of brochure and postage on top of that, you can expect to spend about $1 per item. Before doing a large mailing you should test a list by mailing to a small group first. You can find helpful advice on using direct mail through the U.S. Postal Service publications mentioned earlier in this book. Visit **www.usps.com/businessmail101** and **www.usps.com/directmail/publications.htm**.

Brochures

If you are marketing to businesses, you can get ideas of what to include in your brochure by visiting the websites or getting on the mailing lists of seminar companies (see section 7.3). When preparing your own marketing materials, remember to focus on communicating all the benefits of attending (refer to section 2.5 of this guide if you need a refresher). As well as the information, benefits of attending a seminar may include: a chance to network, personal advice from an expert, or a fun night out.

Among the other items you can include in a brochure:

- Who should attend

- When and where the seminar takes place

- The speaker's credentials

- Testimonials

- That enrollment is limited (mention if past seminars sold out)

- A call to action such as "Register now!"

- How to register, including your phone number and web address

Brochures with this information can also be used to market seminars to the public. The ideal brochure for a public seminar is one that can double as a poster (e.g. printed on one side of a colorful 8½" x 11" sheet). If permitted, try posting them at bookstores and college campuses – two places you're likely to find people interested in seminars.

Buying Advertising

Although advertising is rarely effective for traditional business seminars, it can be an excellent way to market a public seminar.

I suggest starting small. Try a classified or a small display ad in your local newspaper or a newsletter read by your intended audience. Keep in mind that the purpose of your advertising is not to get registrations, it is to get inquiries, so you don't need to include all the details in your ad. Your ad should include a large heading that promises a benefit. In addition to at least one benefit, your ad should give the seminar date, time, cost, and where to get more information. Here's an example:

PUBLISH YOUR BOOK

Find out how you can become a published author at a seminar on Saturday, January 30, from 10 am to 4 pm at the Ramada Hotel Downtown. The last seminar SOLD OUT so register early. Cost $49 (or $39 each if you bring a friend). Call Seminars Un-limited at 555-1212 or visit www.pubseminar.com.

I experimented with running ads up to two months before a seminar, and found the closer to the date an ad was placed, the more effective it was. Now, I usually advertise only in the most well-read issue of the week (the Sunday newspaper in U.S. cities or Saturday in Canadian cities), with the first ad placed two weekends before the event, and another ad placed the weekend immediately before the seminar.

Many seminar presenters fear if they don't give people plenty of notice, their audience will already have other plans by the time they actually see an advertisement. However, some people would not be able to attend if you gave them six months notice. For many seminars, the few registrations you will lose by advertising close to the date are more than offset by those you will gain from people compelled to "take action."

9.5.6   Registering People

If you have plenty of spare time, you could sit by the phone waiting for it to ring. Another option is to speak only with people who are ready to register or who want to speak to you personally.

Give People Written Information

Many people seeking information about a seminar are actually happier to get it in writing to avoid a potential "sales pitch." In your advertising you can direct people to your website, and in your telephone voice mail message you can offer to send information about the seminar by fax, mail, or e-mail.

Although there are a few people who won't leave messages on voice mail, we compared voice mail with having full-time sales staff answer the phones, and found virtually no difference in the number of registrations. However, voice mail is much less expensive!

The information you send people and put on your website could include your brochure, a page of testimonials, and a list of answers to the most frequently asked questions about the seminar. (But do not give details about the seminar's activities, such as games or role plays, if they might potentially scare people off.)

In some cases it will be worth your time to make follow-up phone calls to see if people want to register. However, in our five years of running a seminar company we found it was usually not worth the effort of making follow-up calls for most seminars. If your information effectively communicates the benefits of attending, people will call you to register.

What to Say on the Phone

When speaking to people about the seminar, I suggest the first thing you should ask them is "Are you calling to register for the seminar or do you need more information?" If you start describing the seminar to someone who is calling to register, you might actually talk them out of it! ("Oh I didn't realize you cover that in the seminar ... maybe it's not for me.")

If someone says they want to register, the next words out of your mouth should be "Would you like to put that on VISA or MasterCard?" (Clayton says that should be your first question as soon as someone says they're calling about the seminar. "If they want information, they will let you know," he says.)

> **TIP:** To make it as easy as possible for people to register, make sure you can accept payment by VISA and MasterCard. Contact your bank to become a credit card "merchant."

If the caller says "I need some information," ask "Do you have specific questions or do you want some general information?" If they have specific questions, answer them and don't volunteer additional information until their registration is complete.

To prepare for those who say "Tell me what it's all about," have a script that's about a minute long. Briefly describe what the seminar covers and emphasize benefits of attending. Ask the caller what interested them in the seminar, so you can explain how the seminar will provide what they are looking for. Then ask "Would you like to register?" (A sample script is included on the CD-ROM.)

If someone asks how many people are registered, do not tell them unless you are almost sold out. Numerous seminars sell out after a slow start, but if you tell your caller registrations are slow they will feel no sense of urgency to register. They may even perceive the seminar as a failure and decide against registering. Tell them that although exact registration figures are not available, you still have some seats left, but you're not sure how long they will last.

If you are asked when the next seminar will take place, and you have not scheduled another one, you can truthfully say you don't know if there will be another seminar on this topic. If people are given the option of attending at a later date, you will lose a significant number of registrations.

When someone is ready to register, you will want to find out the registrant's name, contact information, and method of payment. You should also ask how they heard about the seminar so you can monitor the effectiveness of your various marketing activities. Follow up with a confirmation letter to remind them of the date, time and location of the seminar, plus any other information you want them to know such as your cancellation policy.

Your Cancellation Policy

Sooner or later you will hear from someone who wants to cancel their registration. When my partner Clayton and I first started presenting seminars, our refund policy was extremely generous. Someone could cancel the day of the seminar – or simply not show up – and we would give them a full refund.

We thought this would be good for customer relations but we eventually came to the realization that people who cancelled *never* registered again. Not only did we end up returning a significant amount of money, but last-minute cancellations kept us from being able to sell the seats to other people.

The percentage of registrants who will try to cancel at the last minute depends on the level of risk involved in your seminar. While business seminars are relatively low risk, if given the opportunity, one-third of registrants for a singles seminar will try to back out and ask for a full refund (as we learned from our own seminars as well as those sponsored by other organizations).

We found the ideal policy is one requiring 10 days notice of cancellation. Anyone who cancels by this deadline receives a refund less an administrative fee of about 30% of the seminar price (up to $25). If someone tries to cancel fewer than 10 days before the seminar, there is no refund, but they can send someone else to the seminar in their place. In special cases, they can transfer their registration to a future seminar.

Getting Last Minute Registrations

If you run an ad for an inexpensive public seminar ($49 or less) several days before the event, you may get as many as 50% of your registrations from walk-ins – people who show up at the door. But don't count on it! The number of walk-ins depends on the time of day (an evening seminar may get you 10 times as many walk-ins as a full-day seminar), what the weather is like, what else is going on in town that night, the topic of your seminar, and whether or not you answer the telephone on the day of the seminar.

If possible, have voice mail respond to all calls on the day of your seminar. As surprising as it may seem, this may dramatically increase last minute registrations. To encourage walk-ins, your message should invite them to show up.

For example, "If you are calling about the gardening seminar happening tonight at the Ritz Hotel, we are accepting registrations at the door starting at 5:30 p.m. The cost is $49. The address is 345 Main Street." This type of message also helps any of your pre-paid registrants who call because they have forgotten the time or place. (And you won't have to deal with any registrants who are trying to cancel at the last minute.)

If you answer the phone, you may get some registrations, but you will likely lose more. That's because many last minute callers are unsure about attending. When given the chance to talk to someone, most will ask "When is the next seminar on this topic?" No matter what answer you give ("in six months," "not for another 10 years," "never") many will not attend the seminar that day – or ever.

As strange as it may seem, if you do not satisfy their curiosity on this question, many of those who would not show up if you told them the seminar will never be offered again, will show up fearing this may be their last chance to attend!

There may be the odd last minute caller who needs more information before deciding to register. However, most people who are seriously interested will show up at the door even if they still have some questions.

Just as you should avoid answering the phone at your office, you should ask the hotel not to put any calls through to your meeting room – chances are much higher that the caller will be someone trying to cancel their registration rather than someone calling to register. Remember, anyone who is seriously interested will show up at the door. (If you are expecting a call and don't have a cell phone, have the hotel switchboard take messages for you.)

When someone approaches the registration desk, ask if they have pre-registered. If they have not, ask their name and how they would like to pay for the seminar. Most walk-ins are there because they want to attend. Do not assume they need information. (Remember, you might talk them out of it!) If someone asks for information, give them a brochure to read unless you have someone who can answer questions away from the registration desk.

9.5.7 Preparing for the Seminar

To prepare for the seminar you will need to determine what you will need to make it run as smoothly as possible. Your job will be much easier if you prepare a master list of supplies you will need for the seminar, including the following. (See the CD-ROM for a sample checklist.)

- File folder with hotel contract

- Supplies for your registration table

- Participant materials such as handouts

- Instructor's notes and audiovisual materials such as overheads

- Any promotional literature or products to sell at the seminar

Support Staff

You should arrange for support staff to assist you before and during the seminar. Staff can help with tasks such as signing people in at the registration desk, tracking down hotel staff when you need something, distributing handouts, keeping the room temperature comfortable, making sure refreshments are available for breaks, staffing your book table, or anything else that might arise during the seminar.

If your friends or associates are not available to help you, an alternative is to hire a couple of people from a temporary agency or through your local college placement office. Students are often happy to help with a seminar for free, if they can attend at no cost.

Have your registration personnel arrive an hour before the registration desk opens so you can show them how to handle registrations. (They will then be available to assist you with any last-minute room set-up.) Registration might involve having people sign in, giving them their credit card slips, handling any cash payments, giving out nametags and other materials, showing participants to their seats, or directing them to the coat check, coffee station, washrooms, etc.

What to Do When You Arrive

Even if you have personally discussed the room set-up with the catering co-ordinator and faxed a diagram of how you would like everything arranged, you should arrive early to make sure your wishes have been followed. In case changes are needed, allow yourself at least an hour if possible, before the registration desk opens.

Some things to check are:

- Is your seminar listed properly and with the correct start time on the hotel sign boards?

- Is the room layout correct?

- Is all the audio-visual equipment in the room and does it all work properly? (Don't assume it works just because it's there. Make sure you test every piece of equipment.)

- Is the registration desk set up properly?

- Is everything in the room that you have asked for?

If major changes need to be made you should ask for assistance from the hotel staff. You may hear "That wasn't what we were told to do" or "We never got any fax." This is normal. After the grumbling stops, you will likely find the staff are helpful and efficient.

Preparing for Walk-Ins

Since you don't know how many walk-ins may show up, put out enough chairs only for those who have pre-paid. (If there are a lot of empty chairs in the room, it may look like the seminar is not a success.) Stack extra chairs at the back of the room, then, if you need extras, one of your assistants can put them out.

If your event is classroom style, one option is to leave enough room at all the tables to add an extra chair if needed. For example, if a table will comfortably fit three people, you can put two chairs at it, and add a third if your turn-out is larger than expected.

Once your room is set-up and your support staff is ready, it's a good idea to relax for a few minutes before your seminar starts. Then enjoy! Presenting a successful seminar – especially to a paying audience that is eager to hear what you have to say – is a truly rewarding experience.

9.6 Conclusion

You are near the end of the FabJob *Guide to Become a Motivational Speaker*. Hopefully, it is just the beginning of an exciting leap forward in your speaking career.

On the CD-ROM, you will find a variety of samples you can use including a contract, checklists, letters, and even a sample motivational speech. To get the most from this guide, it is recommended that you refer back to the information in this book and CD-ROM as you develop your career. While you may not be ready to implement some of the ideas now, they may be just what you need to give your career a boost at some point in the future.

I sincerely hope you have enjoyed this guide and gained some valuable ideas from it – and that you will be fabulously successful as a speaker and in all areas of your life.

More Guides to Build Your Business

Increase your income by offering additional services. Here are some recommended FabJob guides to help you build your business:

Get Paid to Help People Achieve Success

Imagine having a fulfilling career coaching people how to achieve success in their careers, relationships, and life. In the **FabJob Guide to Become a Life Coach** you will learn:

- How to choose a coaching specialization such as corporate and executive coaching, relationship coaching, or spiritual coaching

- How to help clients identify problems and set goals (includes a sample coaching session, questions to ask clients, and sample coaching exercises to use with individuals and groups)

- How to start and run a part-time or full-time coaching business and get clients (includes a sample client intake form and client contracts)

Get Paid to Give Business Advice

Imagine having a respected, high paying career where executives turn to you for advice on running their business. The **FabJob Guide to Become a Business Consultant** shows you:

- How to carry out a business consulting project step-by-step from conducting a needs analysis to presenting recommendations to the client

- How to get hired by a consulting firm or as an internal consultant for a corporation

- How to start your own consulting business, price your services, and get clients

- How to be certified as a professional business consultant

Visit www.FabJob.com to order guides today!

Get Paid to Help People Look Fabulous

Imagine having an exciting high paying job showing people and companies how to make a fabulous impression.

FabJob Guide to Become an Image Consultant shows you how to:

- Do image consultations and advise people about: total image makeovers, communication skills, wardrobe, and corporate image
- Start an image consulting business, price your services, and find clients
- Select strategic partners such as makeup artists, hair stylists, and cosmetic surgeons
- Have the polished look and personal style of a professional image consultant

Get Paid to Give Etiquette Advice

Imagine having a rewarding career teaching people essential skills they need to succeed in business and in life.

In the **FabJob Guide to Become an Etiquette Consultant** you will learn how to:

- Become an expert in social, dining, business, children's or international etiquette
- Coach individuals on proper etiquette
- Create a part-time or full-time job as an etiquette consultant
- Start an etiquette consulting business, price your services, and find clients
- Present etiquette seminars or workshops and corporate training programs

Visit www.FabJob.com to order guides today!

Save 50% on Your Next Purchase

Would you like to save money on your next FabJob guide purchase? Please contact us at **www.FabJob.com/feedback.asp** to tell us how this guide has helped prepare you for your dream career. If we publish your comments on our website or in our promotional materials, we will send you a gift certificate for 50% off your next purchase of a FabJob guide.

Get Free Career Advice

Get valuable career advice for free by subscribing to the FabJob newsletter. You'll receive insightful tips on: how to break into the job of your dreams or start the business of your dreams, how to avoid career mistakes, and how to increase your on-the-job success. You'll also receive discounts on FabJob guides, and be the first to know about upcoming titles. Subscribe to the FabJob newsletter at **www.FabJob.com/newsletter.asp**.

Does Someone You Love Deserve a FabJob?

Giving a FabJob® guide is a fabulous way to show someone you believe in them and support their dreams. Help them break into the career of their dreams with more than 75 career guides to choose from.

Visit www.FabJob.com to order guides today!